G000150785

Ergodicity.

Definition, Examples, And Implications, As Simple As Possible

Luca Dellanna

@DellAnnaLuca

Luca-dellanna.com

First edition

November 2020

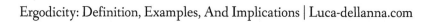

[Page intentionally left blank]

Other books by Luca Dellanna:

Teams Are Adaptive Systems (2020)

The Control Heuristic, First Edition (2020)

Best Practices for Operational Excellence (2019)

100 Truths You Will Learn Too Late (2019)

The Power of Adaptation (2018)

The World Through a Magnifying Glass (2018)

TABLE OF CONTENTS

INTRODUCTION

The reason I didn't spend enough time with my father is that I optimized my life as if he would be there forever.[1] Under that assumption, spending my youth focusing solely on school and friends made sense. I would have had the rest of my life to spend with him. Sadly, he passed away when I was 17, and I got left with a world of regret.

It is human nature to feel torn between maximizing our potential and avoiding regret. Ergodicity will help you understand how to navigate this tension.

---

[1] The "forever" in the text above is, of course, an exaggeration. I meant that I expected my father to live for another few decades. In the US, the average male becomes a father at 31 years old and dies at 78. This means that, on average, a first child will have 47 years to spend with his father. Sadly, this expectation is thwarted by the fact that averages represent not certainties but distributions. many children see their father die younger than they thought – 7% of first-children see their father die before they come of age (Assuming that their father had them at 31 years old, as per the previous data point, and that fathers have the same life expectancy as the average male, and that these distributions are homogeneous. Inhomogeneity will be the object of a later chapter. Source: US Social Security's actuarial table for 2016).

TWO VOICES

We all hear two voices in our heads. One says, "Do not fall behind." This is the voice of social pressure and of our fear of missing out. It makes us work overtime, use all of our salary to buy nice things, and spend our time befriending the coolest or sexiest people around. This voice believes that your short-term success determines your long-term happiness.

The second voice says, "Do not risk what you cannot recover." This is the voice of prudence. It makes us take the safe choice, sacrificing outer-world success for safety. This voice believes that worst-case scenarios prevent you from achieving long-term happiness.

The tricky part is that both voices are right. If you only listen to the first voice, you'll take too many risks, and sooner or later, you will end up broke, alone, or dead. However, if you only listen to the second voice, you will fall so behind that you will also end up broke, alone, or in a dysfunctional state.

The key is to learn when to listen to which voice. In some contexts, you can safely listen to the first one. Maximize your short-term, and the long-term will take care of itself. Conversely, in other contexts, a single negative event can spell your ruin. There, you must listen to both voices at the same time.

Ergodicity is a novel concept that helps you figure out which voice to listen to and which posture to adopt.

ERGODICITY AND IRREVERSIBILITY

The day after children injure themselves or fight with a friend, they're back playing together. Almost none of their mistakes have permanent consequences. Conversely, adults are in a perpetual state of tension because so many of their mistakes have irreversible consequences.[2] **When people say that childhood was the best time of their lives, they usually miss reversibility.**

Childhood is so easy and care-free because children can wholeheartedly listen to the first voice, the one that is all about maximizing the present. Conversely, adults also hear the second one, which is about avoiding ruin.[3] Hearing both voices and not knowing how to balance them is a major source of stress. "Do not fall behind!" and "Do not take risks!" seem so contradictory. We feel they represent incompatible needs.

The truth is that both voices are fully compatible. You can avoid risking what cannot be recovered *and* not fall behind. This book explains how.

(By the way, avoiding to risk what you cannot recover *is* how you get ahead in the long term. The first chapters of this book use the gambler's game of Russian Roulette to explain this contradictory point.)

---

[2] Some readers might be familiar with the book "Finite And Infinite Games" by James P. Carse. After you're done with this book, you might try reading the first part of the Carse's book as if "finite" meant "irreversible" and "infinite players" meant "players in search of ergodicity."

This exercise might help give a spiritual or philosophical meaning to the contents of my book.

[3] Events that make children hear the second voice prematurely are often source of trauma.

ERGODICITY, PAYOFFS, AND THE LONG RUN

The first voice, the one that says, "do not fall behind," takes decisions based on cost-benefit analyses. Whatever brings more benefits than costs, do it.

After all, logically, if you always make the choices with the best trade-offs, you should get ahead, right?

Wrong. **Maximizing the expected returns of your choices is a good strategy only if the consequences of mistakes and misfortunes are reversible. Otherwise, it's a stupid strategy.** The first chapters of this book will show you a few practical examples that justify this point. For the moment, I want to point out the importance of the clause on reversibility. As a first approximation, we can say that **what is optimal in the presence of reversibility is stupid otherwise, and the other way around.**

This whole book and the study of ergodicity in general are mostly about justifying this point. The objective is to give you the arguments to tell the first voice, "yes, I do not want to fall behind, but to do so, I must avoid risks with irreversible consequences," and to tell the second one, "yes, I must avoid some risks, but not all – only those with irreversible consequences."[4]

---

[4] This paragraph leaves out many important considerations. This is just the introduction. The rest of the book gives a more exhaustive description of the study of ergodicity and its purpose.

ABOUT THIS BOOK

If the introduction seemed abstract, do not worry. The next few chapters contain practical examples that explain the impact of ergodicity on our lives. They begin by studying a gambler's game with irreversible consequences, the Russian Roulette. They then show that many components of our daily lives, such as relationships, careers, and investments, follow Russian Roulette rules – not in how they grow, but in how they end.

Later, the first half describes other components of ergodicity theory and culminates with its definition.

The second half of the book comprises three parts, each describing one key strategy you can apply to manage non-ergodicity.

ABOUT FOOTNOTES AND PRECISION

I wrote this book to explain the relevance of ergodicity to readers interested in its practical applications but not in its mathematical foundations.

This book is not a comprehensive guide on ergodicity. Other manuscripts do a better job on the dimensions of precision and theoretical completeness. They are meant for the academic public. Instead, I chose to let a different readership enjoy an understanding of ergodicity.

In the inevitable tradeoff between formal precision and accessibility, I favored the latter. Therefore, this book contains sentences that are correct in their practical meaning but technically imprecise. **I use footnotes to reference justifications and more precise formulations.**

Sometimes, I edited quotes for punctuation. Emphasis is always mine.

If you are a reader who is not versed in mathematics or not interested in the theory behind the practice, you can skip the footnotes or read them after having finished the book. Instead, if you already know about ergodicity, you might find interest, clarity, and completeness in them.

Either way, enjoy this book!

ACKNOWLEDGMENTS

This book wouldn't have seen the light without the previous work on ergodicity of many scholars. Nassim Nicholas Taleb, who wrote the books that brought the topic to my attention, Ole Peters, who perhaps more than anyone else advanced the understanding of this topic, Alexander Adamou, Murray Gell-Mann, Ed Thorp, John Larry Kelly Jr., and all the other scholars who worked on the topic. This book stands on the shoulders of giants. The end of this book contains a selected list of their works.

DISCLAIMER

Always use common sense. Nothing in this book is financial advice or advice of any other kind. The author shall not be held liable for the application or misapplication of the contents of this book. You can find a link to my full disclaimer at **Luca-dellanna.com**

Part 1

LOSSES ABSORB FUTURE GAINS

Ever since a young age, we are taught that a cost-benefit analysis determines whether it is a good idea to do something. If the gains are larger than the losses, then you can go ahead.

The real world begs to differ. There are cases in which it is a terrible idea to do something whose gains are larger than its losses.[5] The next chapter tells the story of how my cousin learned this lesson during his short-lived career as a professional skier.

---

[5] This applies to "Russian Roulette" situations – a concept explained in the chapter after the next.

CHAPTER 1.1
IT IS NOT THE FASTEST SKIER THAT WINS RACES

My cousin was born in a mountain village in the French Alps. Like many there, he learned to ski before reading. I am a good skier, but I remember the humiliation when I was 14 and he was 6, seeing him surpass me, swift as a bullet. At a young age, he made it into the World Championships for his age bracket. Boy, he was fast.

His career came to an abrupt end a decade later, one injury at a time. First, he injured his ankle. Then, he broke his knee. A few more injuries later, he retired, too young. From him, I learned that the skiers that you see on TV, the fastest racers in the world, didn't get there because they were the fastest.

They got there because they were the fastest of those who didn't get injured into retirement.

In skiing, and life in general, **it is not the best ones who succeed. It is the best ones of those who survive.**

CHAPTER 1.2
PERFORMANCE VS. SURVIVAL

In theory, performance determines success. The fastest skier wins the race, and the most performing employee becomes the most successful one.

In practice, **performance is subordinate to survival**. It is the fastest racer of those who survive that wins races, it is the most performing employee who doesn't burn out that becomes the most successful, and so on.

I'm not just making the banal point that survival matters. I'm saying that it matters *more than performance*.[6] On the next page, let's run the numbers.

---

[6] I'm not saying that speed or performance doesn't matter. It does. It just matters less than survival, given a long enough time to reach success (whatever its definition).

Let's imagine that every time my cousin participates in a skiing race, he has a two-in-ten chance of winning it, and a two-in-ten chance of breaking his knee.[7] How many races will he have won, on average, at the end of a championship consisting of 10 races?

The naïve answer is two races. That is the product of the number of races, 10, times the probability of winning each, two-in-ten. This would be correct if the races were independent of each other. However, in reality, if he breaks his knee during a race, he misses the following ones.

So, he can participate in the second race only if he didn't break his knee during the first one. He can participate in the third race only if he didn't break his knee in the previous two ones, and so on. His chances of completing all ten races are pretty slim – only 11%.[8] If we take the time to compute his chances to participate in each race, we discover that his expected number of wins is less than one.[9] This is fewer than the two wins we would expect if breaking a knee didn't prevent him from participating in subsequent races.

The point is, **in a single instant of time, pure performance is all that matters. Instead, over a prolonged period of time, survival dwarfs performance.**

---

[7] Of course, this odds are greatly exaggerated, to show the point more clearly.

[8] That would be 80% (the chances of safely completing a race) to the power of 10 (the number of races).

[9] The expected number of wins is $\sum (0.8^i \cdot 0.2)$, with i ranging from 1 to 10, where 0.8 is the chances of ending the race without an injury, and 0.2 are the chances of winning it. The result is 0.71 expected wins.

WE CAN ONLY OBSERVE THE LONG-TERM OUTSIDE OF THE SHORT-TERM

There is a difference between what matters when we consider narrow intervals and what does when we consider broader ones. **Over the short term, consequences that apply beyond the short-term do not matter. Over the long term, they do.**

In my cousin's case, the broken leg preventing him from competing in future races is the "phantom consequence" that is not observable in the short term but affects the long term. If we make decisions based on what happens over narrow intervals and forget about these "phantom consequences," we will make bad decisions.[10] Ergodicity is the study of these phantom consequences.[11]

---

[10] Good ideas make for the worst mistakes.

[11] Also.

IRREVERSIBILITY ABSORBS FUTURE GAINS

The explanation for the skier paradox is that, whereas my cousin had a chance to win each race, he is not guaranteed to race all of them. Any major injury prevents him from participating, causing him to forego future gains.

In general, we can say that in any repeated activity, **irreversibility absorbs future gains.** This means that you cannot extrapolate future outcomes from solely the expected outcomes of the activity performed once.

SUSTAINED PERFORMANCE

Of course, what I mentioned so far is about long-term performance, not short-term one. However, in many venues of life, the two are more similar than apparent.

For example, winning a single race is an instance of short-term performance. A good racer can just "risk it all" and win, with a bit of luck. However, to become good enough a racer to do it, long-term performance is necessary too.

Too often, we observe a snapshot of someone's life and believe that we witnessed a piece of short-term performance. But if skills are required even to attempt performing that, then what we are really observing is long-term performance.

PRACTICAL APPLICATIONS

If you practice yoga, do not attempt to reach the maximum amount of stretch per session.[12] Instead, maximize the amount you can achieve without risking any major injury.[13] One is enough to prevent you from practicing effectively for months or even years.

If you are a salesperson, do not attempt to make the most sales this quarter. Instead, sell as much as you can without risking your reputation and your brand's.

If you have a job, do not attempt to work as hard as possible. Instead, work as hard as you can without risking your health, marriage, or mental sanity. These three are damn hard to recover once lost.[14]

More in general, in any endeavor in which success depends on you accumulating some kind of resource (money, skill, connections, trust[15], etc.), **do not maximize growth regardless of survival. Instead, maximize growth that conserves survival.**

---

[12] Yes, I know, yoga is much more than stretching. This paragraph is for those who focus on the physical part.

[13] Or, better and wiser, focus on getting the input right rather than on maximizing the output.

[14] This doesn't mean that hard work is bad. It's not. Small stretches of extreme hard work are good and, in some professions, necessary. The problem is when there is no time for recovery, and damage accumulates until the inevitable breakdown.

[15] Trust takes years to create and seconds to destroy, they say. True, but it also misses the point that **trust takes personal closeness to create – if you break the trust someone put into you, you might be denied that closeness and thus the chances to rebuild trust.**

THE SWEET SPOT

The above is not an invitation to excessive prudence. Yes, until you experience pain, you do not know where the boundary is. And yes, going too slowly comes with problems too. Rather, this is an invitation to **distinguish between calculated risks whose consequences you can recover from and recklessness whose consequences might permanently debilitate you. There is a sweet spot where you expose yourself to the former but not the latter[16] – that's a good place to aim.**

Of course, it's easier said than done. Moreover, some people feel such a strong desire to achieve a risky goal that they might feel that not doing it would permanently debilitate them. It's fine. This book wants to be informative, not prescriptive. It aims at giving you the tools to make informed decisions, not at making decisions for you.

THE PATH FORWARD

So far, I've talked about irreversibility in a rather abstract way. The next chapter presents a quantifiable example: Russian Roulette.

---

[16] Depending on the domain, in absolute terms, or relatively to the minimum reasonably possible to conduct the activity.

CHAPTER 1.3
RUSSIAN ROULETTE

If you are reading this book, you probably never played Russian Roulette. It is a gambler's game of the riskiest kind. The player takes a gun, empties the cylinder, and puts back a single bullet. Then, he spins the cylinder to randomize the position of the bullet. Finally, he takes the gun to his head. After staring at death for a few seconds, he pulls the trigger. If he survives, he collects a prize, usually in the tens of thousands of dollars. (Obviously, do not try this at home, or anywhere else.)

The reason I'm writing about Russian Roulette is that some people are terrible at judging its odds. They then apply the same mistake to other areas of their life, such as their relationships or careers, with disastrous consequences. Let's see if you can guess better than them.

Usually, the game is played with a six-holes cylinder. This means that when the player pulls the trigger, he has a one-in-six chance of dying and a five-in-six chance of winning. Let's imagine that the prize for a win is $6,000. How much money are you expected to win if you play Russian Roulette once?

The right answer is $5,000. That is the prize, $6,000, multiplied by the chances of winning, five-in-six. Now, a harder question. **How much are you expected to win if you play Russian Roulette a hundred times?**

A back-of-the-napkin calculation would yield $500,000. That would be $5,000 (the expected winnings for a single play) multiplied by 100 (the number of plays). However, this answer is wrong.

The correct answer is $0. After 100 rounds of Russian Roulette, you're almost certainly dead and unable to collect any winning.[17]

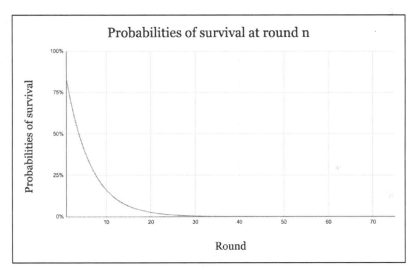

Probabilities of survival at round n

---

[17] You only have a 12-in-a-billion chance of surviving 100 rounds of Russian Roulette.

For comparison, you have a 16% chance of surviving 10 rounds and a 1% chance of surviving 25 rounds.

In general, your chances of survival are $(5/6)^n$, where 5/6 are your chances of surviving one round, and n is the number of rounds played. Death over time is certain, that is, $(5/6)^n$ tends to zero for $n \to \infty$.

The chart below shows you the expected returns after playing Russian Roulette multiple times. As you can see, returns quickly plummet.

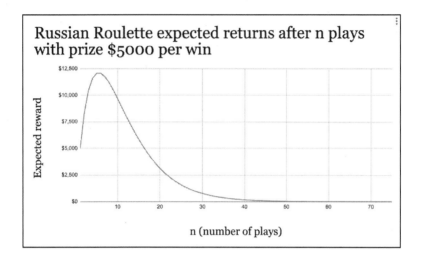

In particular, in the first part of the curve, returns increase. For example, after two plays, you win double the money but only decrease your chances of survival by one-in-six compared to playing once.

However, after a bit, the returns stall. For example, by playing a sixth time, your winnings in case of survival become 6x instead of 5x, a 6/5 multiplier, but your chances of survival decrease by one-in-six, a 5/6 multiplier. The two multipliers are reciprocal, so they cancel each other.

After that, the returns decrease. For example, by playing a seventh time, your winnings in case of survival become 7x instead of 6x, a 7/6 multiplier, but your chances of survival still decrease by one-in-six, a 5/6 multiplier. 7/6 multiplied 5/6 makes 35/36, which is lower than one, so returns decrease. Afterward, it's all downhill. 40/42, 45/48, 50/54, …

The previous thought experiment comes from Nassim Nicholas Taleb's "Skin In The Game" and clearly shows the link between ergodicity and irreversibility.

People who replied "$500,000" to the previous question assumed that death in one round just means that no winnings are collected during that round, but future rounds are still winnable. In Russian Roulette, however, one loss means that you also forego all future gains. Losses are irreversible and extend in the future.

Sadly, relationships, careers, investments, and sports often share this undesirable property. For example, relationships are like Russian Roulette in the sense that they grow stronger over time, but only if you get to spend time with your partner. If, one day, you break their trust, they might decide not to see you again. You will lose all chances to rebuild the relationship.

Similarly, in investing, losing your capital means that you lost both your capital *and* all future returns that it could have generated.

THE PATH FORWARD

If you feel slightly confused, do not worry. It's normal. Irreversibility is counterintuitive and goes against what we usually learned in school – that averages matter equally in the short- and in the long-term. This is seldom true. The next chapter explains why.

CHAPTER 1.4
THE LAW OF LARGE NUMBERS

If you flip a coin, it will come out half of the time as heads, and half of the time as tails. This is true if you flip it infinite times. However, if you only flip it ten times, it may come up six times as heads and four times as tails – a different result than the five and five expected. The fewer the flips, the higher the chances that the tally differs from the expected 50%.

We notice that the average of observed results converges to the expected value as a larger number of trials is performed. This is called *the law of large numbers*.

We generally assume the law of large numbers to be always relevant. In reality, it seldom is for individuals. It requires, well, a large number of trials. The problem is that in most real-life situations, we have a limited number of trials. For example, I cannot keep picking risky stocks until I get rich – a few bad results in a row, and I am broke.

Whenever an activity cannot be assumed repeatable at infinity, we should be wary of expecting to achieve its average outcome.

GAME-OVER

In Russian Roulette, your expected earnings per trigger pulled are $5,000. However, if you're unable to pull it because you're dead, your future earnings are effectively $0. You can only keep playing to win more money if you're alive.

Any form of "game-over" nullifies future gains, bringing the average down. Hence, we can say that possible game-overs are a cause of non-ergodicity.

Similarly, in my cousin's example, breaking his leg is a form of game-over (the damage is irreversible, at least during the championship). It implies losing the race in which the injury took place *and* all the following ones. This causes his average number of wins during a championship to be lower than expected (his chances of winning a race multiplied by the number of races).

MANY KINDS OF GAME-OVER

Game-overs are common. They include bankruptcies, injuries, severe depressions, burnouts, and break-ups of all kinds (between romantic partners, business partners, or friends).

The next chapter analyzes some of them.

CHAPTER 1.5

MUCH OF LIFE IS A RUSSIAN ROULETTE

The last two chapters put a lot of emphasis on the mechanics of Russian Roulette. You might have been wondering, "Great, but I'm not a gambler. Why should I care about Russian Roulette?"

The thing is, much of life follows similar mechanics, in which losses absorb future gains. I already mentioned how, in relationships, breaking trust might prevent any future attempt to rebuild the relationship. Here are a couple more examples.

- **Sports.** The harder you practice, the faster you progress. However, if you try too hard, you might injure yourself. Irrecoverable damage at your joints might end your ability to perform the sport well, or at all.

- **Career.** The harder you work, the more chances you have for professional success. However, if you work too many hours for too long, you might endanger your health, marriage, or mental sanity. Once lost, these are hard, if not impossible, to recover.

A single negative event can render short-term maximization irrelevant.

PRUDENCE, NOT COWARDICE

The presence of irreversibility doesn't imply that you should not take any risk.[18] Instead, it means that you should acknowledge the non-ergodicity of the context at hand and take risks in a way that does not seriously impair your life if things go wrong.

Prudence, not cowardice.

---

[18] It's risky not to take risks.

CHAPTER 1.6

POPULATION AND LIFETIME OUTCOMES

Earlier on, I introduced the gambler's game of Russian Roulette. As a reminder, a player has a one-in-six chance of dying and a five-in-six chance of winning a prize, let's say $6,000.

In Russian Roulette, the outcome you get by playing it a few times is different from the average outcome of a few people playing it once. Let's compute each.

Let's say that six people play Russian Roulette once each. The prize is $6,000. On average, one person will die and five will win $6,000. The group as a whole obtained one death and $30,000. Divided by the number of participants, 6, it makes 1/6 of a death and $5,000. That is **the expected outcome.**

This expectation remains correct if we increase the number of gamblers. With 600 gamblers, you will have an average of 100 deaths and $3M. Divided by 600 people, it still makes 1/6 of a death and $5,000. Therefore, the expected outcome is also called **the population outcome**[19]

---

[19] Sometimes also called the *ensemble average.*

Your individual expected outcome if you play Russian Roulette once is also 1/6 of a death and $5,000. However, if you play it more than once, it begins to decrease. If you play it an infinite amount of times, you will be dead for sure. Your final outcome, what you can walk away with, is $0 and a hole in your head.

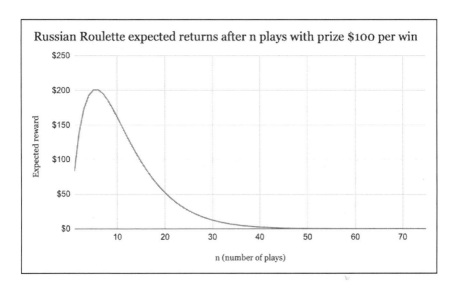

The chart shows how your expected financial gains from playing Russian Roulette many times are roughly zero. I call this expectation, measured across one person and many repetitions, **the lifetime outcome.** Its technical name is *time average* or *time probability*.[20]

---

[20] I use the term "lifetime outcome," even though not canonical, as I have experienced it leading to faster understanding.

I spent a few pages describing the difference between population and lifetime outcomes because they are the key to defining ergodicity. In particular,

A system is ergodic [21] **if its population outcome coincides with the lifetime outcome of each of its components. Otherwise, it is non-ergodic.**

THE PRACTICAL IMPLICATION

The practical implication is that **in ergodic systems, you can use the population outcome to make optimal decisions. In non-ergodic systems, you cannot.** [22]

For example, Russian Roulette is non-ergodic because the lifetime outcome differs from the population outcome. If you decide to keep playing it because you fail to grasp its non-ergodicity and mistakenly believe that your lifetime outcome equals your population one, you will end up dead.

Hence the purpose of this book. By teaching you about the implications of non-ergodic contexts and how to recognize them, I hope to help you avoid irreversible mistakes whose importance is sadly clear only after the fact. A bit like my cousin learned with his injury or like I learned when my father passed away.

---

[21] Across this book, I use the expression "a system is ergodic" as a shorthand for "a model describing a system is ergodic". The later chapter on the definition of ergodicity explains this choice.

[22] In an only partially related note, I often joke that 5 in 6 economists think that Russian Roulette is safe.

CHAPTER 1.7
RISK AVERSION

There is a common belief that people are irrationally risk-averse. This belief is the result of experiments such as the following.

"Here is a game. You flip a coin. If it's heads, I give you $1000. If it's tails, you give me $950. Do you want to participate?"

From a logical-naïve point of view, the expected returns of playing the bet is $1000 times 50% (the chances of winning) minus $950 times 50% (the chances of losing). That makes $500 - $475 = $25. On average, every time you play the game, you're expected to win $25. This makes the gamble apparently desirable.

And yet, if researchers go around asking the question to real people, most decline. This led behavioral economists to conclude that people are irrationally risk-averse.

Are they, though?[23]

---

[23] Cunning readers might have thought that such a bet is suspicious. Whoever proposes it must be a swindler, hence it's wise to decline playing. This is a sound reasoning.

However, as the next page will show, even assuming full good faith in the person proposing the bet, it is still advised to refuse playing it.

If people had infinite cash, they could play the game as long as they want. The law of large numbers would kick in, their lifetime outcome would converge to their expected outcome, and they would realize the expected win of $25 per coin flipped.

However, real people do not have infinite cash. They can only play this game a few times before emptying their bank accounts or having to quit the game. Some cannot even afford to lose once.

For real people, the limitation on the number of times they can play can transform their lifetime outcome of a gamble to negative.

The next page shows an example.

Imagine that you have a prosperous sum of $1000 in your pocket. After one iteration of the game,

- you might have won the toss and won $1000.

- you might have lost the toss and lost $950.

The average is a win of $25, as expected. However, if you are offered to play a second time, you can only afford to play if you won the first toss. Therefore, you can expect to win $25 from the second toss only if you won the first one. This means that in four parallel universes,

- In the first, you won both tosses, and you're up by $2000.

- In the second, you won the first toss and lost the second one. You're up $50.

- In the third, you lost the first toss and cannot play again. You're down $950.

- In the fourth, you also lost the first toss and cannot play again. You're down $950.

After two iterations of the game, you're only won an average of: ($2000 + $50 - $950 -$950) / 4 = $37.5

This is surprising! If you had infinite wealth, you would have won an average of $25 per bet times two equals $50. But because your wealth is finite, your average win is less: only $37.5

More importantly, you have a one-in-four chance to win a lot of money, one-in-four chances to win a modest amount, and one-in-two chances of losing a significant amount.[24]

This means that you have a one-in-two chance of being yelled at by your spouse and/or hurt in your self-esteem in exchange for a mere $37.5 expected winnings[25]. Not a choice that any rational person would take.

Actually, it would be idiotic to volunteer to play a game with these odds. The behavioral economists who called for "irrational risk-aversion" are the irrational ones.

Further readings: Ole Peters' papers contain additional examples of how (non-)ergodicity explains the hidden rationality of some risk aversion and of other behaviors that would be irrational in an ideal ergodic world. As far as I know, he was the first to propose ergodicity as the solution to many otherwise puzzling behaviors.

---

[24] If you looked at what happens in time beyond two bets, to three, four, five, and so on, you would notice the following. You would still have a one-in-two chances of losing a significant amount. You would have a smaller and smaller chance of winning a larger and larger amount. And, in the rest of cases, you would win a modest amount.

[25] Assuming a limit of two plays and $1000 cash in the wallet before beginning the game. The more the plays, the lower the average winnings.

CHAPTER 1.8

WHAT YOU SEE IS NOT ALL THERE IS

Deep down, we already know that survival matters. Our instincts scream not to go down the hill that fast, not to work overtime every day risking a burnout, and not to risk betraying the trust of those on which we depend.

Sadly, when we observe someone's success, our automatic reaction is often to desire it for ourselves, without asking ourselves if we would actually like it – both its pros *and its cons*, without cherry-picking.

AngelList founder Naval Ravikant wisely notes that envy is most often an illusion. "The part of the person that we envy doesn't exist without the rest of that person," he writes. "If we aren't willing to trade places with them completely – their life, their body, their thoughts – then there is nothing to be envious about."

I would add that **it is also pointless to envy someone with whom you wouldn't trade places in all parallel universes** – including those in which his gambles didn't pay off. For example, an entrepreneur whose venture had slim chances to succeed.[26]

Do you desire to take his gambles, or do you only desire the winning outcome?

Do not envy the survivors of ventures in which you didn't participate.

---

[26] In this case, it's useful to distinguish the case of an entrepreneur who succeeds against all odds because others were wrong in guessing the odds, and the case of one who took a bet that heavily relied on luck. In the second case, I do not want to take away any merit – society benefits from entrepreneurs taking gambles, so I'm grateful for his actions. However, I am also wary of envying him – I can envy his decision if and only if I would desire to take the gamble he took, not just his win.

SURVIVORSHIP BIAS

Michigan truck driver Mark Clark won four millions at the lottery. Twice, in 2017 and 2020.

Does it make him the greatest investor ever?

It is hard to make the highest returns than the man who won the lottery twice. That doesn't mean that his strategy is worth imitating.

Too often, when we look at the winner, we fail to see all his clones in the parallel universes in which he lost his bets. Any serious decision-making process cannot discard them.

Whenever we desire an outcome because we see those that benefited from it, it is good practice asking yourself, **do you want the outcome, or do you want the opportunity to take the gamble that produced the outcome?** If you only want the former but not the latter, you might be unprepared for what's to come.

CHAPTER 1.9
THE POINT SO FAR

Here are a few key points covered so far:

- Irreversibility absorbs future gains.

- The population outcome is the outcome of many people performing an action once. The lifetime outcome is the outcome of one person performing an action many times.

- If the population and lifetime outcomes differ, the system that produces them is non-ergodic.

- You can only rely on expected outcomes if you are guaranteed a large number of repetitions. Otherwise, they are misleading. (The law of large numbers requires a large number of repetitions).

- Risk aversion is rational in the presence of non-ergodicity.

Part 2

WHAT WORKS ON AVERAGE CAN STILL FAIL LOCALLY

In the first part of this book, we saw the surprising fact that the rules and odds of the Russian Roulette do not change over time, and yet your payoff does. Due to irreversibility, losses absorb future gains.

You learned that what happens in the short term does not necessarily describe what happens in the long term, *even if the conditions do not change over time.*

THE PATH FORWARD

First, we will extend the concept of irreversibility through space. We will see how, for example, a public service might work well on average and yet fail locally.

Then, we will extend irreversibility through the layers of society. We will examine the relationship between you and any group you might be a part of – your family, your company, or your community. You will learn that, even if your incentives are perfectly aligned, and you care for them, and they care for you, "doing the best for their survival" is different from "doing the best for your survival."

Finally, we will move to the third part of this book, where you will receive a definition of ergodicity.

CHAPTER 2.1
ONE VS. MANY

I live in Turin, Italy. It's a quiet metropolis at the foot of the mountains. From there, it's a short ride to Bergamo province, the hardest-hit by the 2020 coronavirus pandemic. So many people died there because the hospitals got overwhelmed. Many perished in their houses because they couldn't access tests and therapies.

And yet, *on average,* the healthcare system worked great. *On average,* hospitals didn't see many coronavirus hospitalizations. On the worst day of the pandemic, only about 10% of Italian public hospital beds were occupied by coronavirus patients.[27]

Of course, average data does not tell us the full story. If every hospital in Italy had 10% of their beds occupied by patients, it wouldn't have been so bad. The problem is that the patients predominantly lived in the same region. A few hospitals got completely overwhelmed, while those in other regions didn't.

A system can work well on average and still fail locally.

---

[27] 29,010 COVID hospitalizations on the 4th of April in Italy, according to statista.com (link), and 284,713 public hospital beds in Italy according to an untitled report on the Italian Health Ministry website (link).

THE ASSUMPTION OF INDEPENDENCE

The law of large numbers says that, as the number of trials increases, the average outcome converges to the expected one. We saw that this applies to ergodic contexts only. In non-ergodic ones, irreversibility limits the number of trials, thus preventing the law of large numbers from applying.

Similarly, we can extend the law of large numbers and its limitations not only through time but also through space and populations.[28] The law of large numbers expects that the larger a population of people performing an action, the closer the average outcome is to the expected average. For example, 75% heads is not a surprising outcome if four people flip a coin (three people flipped head and one flipped tails). However, if four hundred people flip a coin, the average outcome is much more likely to be 50%, or 51%, or some percentage around that.

This happens because the coin results are independent. Your neighbor's result does not influence yours. However, in most of real life, what occurs to your neighbors does influence what happens to you.

For example, we can expect the victims of pandemics and natural disasters to be located near each other. Therefore, we cannot assess whether the emergency systems are ready for such events based on national averages alone. Instead, we must consider local workload spikes.

---

[28] Informally.

On the news, we saw the pain of the families in the hardest-hit areas. People died because the overcrowded local hospitals couldn't admit them.

As an individual, you do not care whether the system works on average. You care if it works for you.

Averages hide local spikes in irreversibility; survival is based on the local.

A test on how much time it takes to get an ambulance on average to reach a patient gives you little information on how long it takes for two ambulances to reach the same point.

CENTRALIZATION

This tension between what happens on average and what happens locally is the main problem of centralization. Centralized organizations such as the WHO or the EU are not omniscient nor have illimited bandwidth. Their executives cannot read tons of data that describe every corner of the world. They must rely on averages. They cannot make thousands of micro-decisions, each appropriate for a given corner of the world. They must take a single, one-fits-all decision.[29] Even if these decisions work on average, they might have a terrible impact on some local populations.[30]

This problem is further compounded by the fact that central organizations tend to receive more input and feedback from people geographically, socially, or culturally close to them. Those living at the geographic, social, or cultural peripheries are often ignored or underweighted by central organizations.

---

[29] I have described some of WHO's policies "minimum common denominator healthcare," due to their tendency to condemn effective measures such as face masks that cannot be applied everywhere due to a lack of resources.

[30] In an ergodic world, institutions such as the EU make much more sense than in a non-ergodic one.

Centralization is only efficient to the central observer. The closer someone lives to the capital, and the more his culture and social status match those of the governors, the more he will be approving of it.

This is not only due to partisanship or collaboration. The closer geographically, socially, and culturally your governors are to you, the more likely they are to work on what you care.[31]

PRACTICAL APPLICATIONS

Be wary of centralization, especially when there is no skin in the game[32] ensuring that the incentives of the center coincide with those of the peripheries.[33] Good intentions and being part of the same country or organization are not enough. Even assuming good faith and competence, the center cannot possibly fathom all consequences of its actions on the periphery, nor it has any good way to measure that in a non-superficial way.

---

[31] Many disagreements between people in good faith come from one of the following two causes. One, they're optimizing different metrics. Two, they're considering the marginal utility of a resource whose utility is nonlinear and of which they possess different quantities (example: $100 are less important to a millionaire than to a single parent working a part-time job – of course they will have different perceptions of the value of $100, even if none is virtue signaling).

[32] Skin in the game will be the object of a further chapter.

[33] The idea of electing representatives of the periphery to become part of the center was supposed to solve the problem. It would, in theory, but only if the representatives were true members of the periphery and, after a short mandate, had to come back and be a member of the periphery again. Sadly, I am witnessing more and more that the representatives elected in the peripheries are members of the center – not geographically but socially and culturally.

GRANULARITY

A major problem of centralization is the lack of granularity. A central government cannot possibly review granular data and cannot enact policies that are granular enough to be effective everywhere. Instead, we get one-fits-all.

Hence the importance of bringing down decision making closer to the people involved. For example, if a decision can be taken at the province or state level, it should be taken at the province level.

Decisions taken at lower levels seem to lack efficiency due to economies of scale but more than make it up with the benefits of tailoring. They provide more of what would be good for the province and less of what would be bad.

CHAPTER 2.2
THE AVERAGE RETURNS AREN'T YOUR RETURNS

Did you ever miss a plane because the train to the airport was late?

It happened to me. The train company telling me that trains are only one minute late on average didn't bring me any relief. I did not care about how late a train is on average. I only cared about the fact that *my train* was late.

Moreover, I did not even care about whether the average delay is one minute or ten. I only cared about the fact that the one time the train was late half an hour, I missed my plane.

Averages are misleading. As we already saw, **systems might work on average and still fail locally.**

IRREVERSIBILITY

Averages are a meaningful metric only when future gains offset past losses. It is often not the case. Continuing the previous example, I do not care if, next time, the train arrives 30 minutes in advance. It certainly doesn't make it up for the fact that last time, a late train made me miss my plane. I do not get a free flight when the train arrives in advance.

As a rule of thumb, **we cannot rely on averages whenever there is a possibility for irreversible damage**[34]. **This is because the possibility of irreversible damage makes a context non-ergodic.**

When we consider averages, the good offsets the bad. However, for individuals, something good happening to someone else doesn't offset the bad that happened to them.[35]

---

[34] Readers versed in ergodicity will know that it's not just about damage, but any forms of irreversibility.

[35] This point is in addition to the previous one that irreversibility absorbs future gains. A bankrupt investor loses the possibility to benefit from the following market growth. And a divorced husband loses the possibility to restore the relationship.

PRACTICAL APPLICATIONS

If you find yourself in a non-ergodic context, do not focus on population-wide averages. Care about *your* outcome, not the average one.

When losses are irreversible, or when losses preclude future gains, do not decide based on averages.

Instead, use more granular data. Ask yourself what might happen *to you*. Ask yourself if and how unexpected losses can negate your future plans.

For example, do not invest all your money in the one investment with the highest average return. Instead, consider what would happen in case of a downturn. Do not care about average returns – only about those with which you could end up.

CHAPTER 2.3

THE GAMBLER AND THE GAMBLE

How to make money in the start-up business?

If you are an investor, the go-to strategy is the following. Place many bets by investing in a lot of promising companies. Push them to grow as fast as possible. Many will fail. A couple will become the next Facebook. The one or two "big wins" will make hundreds of times your money back, recouping the losses on all the other companies, and leaving you with enough profits to drink Mai Tais on a beach for the rest of your life.

That's a great strategy to make money in the start-up business, *for wealthy investors.* Not so much for founders. Many would prefer a strategy where they are likely to end up in full control of a healthy company, rather than a lottery ticket to be the next Zuckerberg.

Of course, it's not so black and white. Many founders do make good money, live exciting years, and make experience and connections. The point is, **the best strategy depends on whether you are the gambler or the gamble.** If you are the gambler, you do not care about each gamble making money. You care about the aggregate of all gambles making money. Conversely, if you are the gamble (in this example, the founder), you do not care about the overall outcome of all gambles but only yours.

YOU: A GAMBLER

Even if you do not play gambling games, it might be useful to see yourself as a gambler. After all, each of your habits is a gamble in which you bet time and energy for a possible return. Similarly, any belief of yours is a gamble. Any job of yours, any relationship of yours, any idea, any decision – they are all investments of time and money in exchange for a future return.

You might be tempted to strive to win any single gamble of yours. Don't. You can afford to let go of a few losing ones.[36] **Their survival is not necessary for yours.**[37]

Remember, the best strategy for the gamble isn't necessarily the best strategy for the gambler.[38]

---

[36] Of course, within the boundaries of ethics, respect, promises, and human decency.

[37] Careful, though, on whether your survival is necessary to theirs. This is one of the reasons I'm skeptical of the idea of managing a country as if it were a company. When you manage a company, you do not have to hire every applicant, and employees can decide to leave and find themselves another company. Conversely, citizens cannot find themselves another country. Some can, but they are a minority. It shouldn't be an obligation or an "or else".

[38] An additional consideration to the example from the previous page is that entrepreneurs (the gamble) can become themselves a gambler if they can withstand failure and quickly make another bet. That's an extremely desirable trait.

REPLACEABLE, FOR WHOM?

This chapter made the point that parties sharing a stake in the same venture might have different incentives. They might have different opinions on what is replaceable and what is not.

This pattern is everywhere in nature and society. For an employee, his career and health are irreplaceable, but for the company, most employees are replaceable. Firings and employee burnouts are part of doing business.[39]

For a mother, her child is irreplaceable. Instead, for the species, natural selection means an improvement.

For a soldier, his life and those of his squad brothers are irreplaceable. For a general, losing a few soldiers is a painful cost that might be worth paying to win the war.

This pattern also applies more figuratively. Your beliefs fight[40] with all their strength to prove their validity and stay in your mind. In contrast, you might benefit from losing a few of them, those that are bringing pain to your life.

---

[39] Of course, we must here ask ourselves the question, for whom? If not for the company, for some of its managers. Employees burning out are generally bad for the company, for not only it loses talent, but it also lowers morale and has other negative indirect effects. However, some managers might be immune to them.

[40] Of course, they do not literally fight – that's just a confabulation explained in my book, "The Control Heuristic."

In general, **the survival of a population does not coincide with the survival of its members, not all of them.**[41]

Of course, this applies to some contexts only. We can call them "non-ergodic." This is not a complete nor precise definition of ergodicity. However, it is a valuable one, for it provides an important distinction. In non-ergodic contexts, you cannot be idealistic and believe that your survival coincides with that of your company or country. You must take additional steps to take care of yourself.

For example, I have many friends working in the consulting business. Their job is hard. Their employers squeeze every bit of productivity out of them. Most went through a burnout. It is to be expected. Their company has little to lose from their burnout, or anyway less than they do. Their incentives are not as aligned as it seems, even though the employees are part of the company, and both value survival.

The question is, does non-ergodicity apply to the relationship between them and their company? Yes. Then, they must acknowledge that they and their company might have different incentives. They must take one of two actions. One, realign incentives – for example, by becoming irreplaceable. Two, acknowledge that they need a plan B.

---

[41] Readers familiar with Nassim Nicholas Taleb's concept of *Antifragility* might have noticed a link. The antifragile increases its chances of survival when some of its components get damaged (not too many, but enough to trigger an antifragile reaction).

This is not about ethics. The point is that a population doesn't have, by default, an incentive for the survival of all of its members. Even if the population means good for its members – especially so. A population must first and foremost ensure its survival to guarantee the survival of its members. And if the survival of the population doesn't coincide with the survival of all its members – as is the case in non-ergodic conditions –, a well-meaning population won't necessarily guarantee the survival of all its members. It won't do so when it comes to the cost of its own survival. For example, when facing external threats that put at risk the survival of the population as a whole, some sacrifices might become necessary. Or, as another example, when the survival of the most decadent or freeloading members of the society might endanger its existence.[42]

---

[42] For a company or a population, replaceability of its members means ergodicity. For the individual members, the opposite applies.

THE IMPLICATION

As an individual, you cannot blindly rely on membership of a group for your survival. Instead, you can become an irreplaceable part of it. This way, the population deems your loss irrecoverable and must take action to prevent it *at all costs*.[43]

BURN YOUR HABITS BEFORE THEY BURN YOU

Natural selection benefits populations. This is good news if you are a population and bad news if you are one of its weak members.

In the latter case, you can turn the tables by making natural selection work for you rather than against you. The trick is to become a population yourself. This is easier than it seems. After all, you already are a population: of habits and beliefs. If you let the feedback you receive from your environment hurt the habits and beliefs that are holding you back, **you are effectively making natural selection act inside you rather than on you.** You become stronger rather than extinct.

You are not your habits nor your beliefs. You are their container. Their survival is not yours. What's best for them might or might not be what's best for you.

---

43 Even though the population is still non-ergodic, any measurement of "survival" on a sample that includes you becomes similar to any sample of the population, so that ergodicity is satisfied for what concerns you and your membership to that population.

CHAPTER 2.4
THE POINT SO FAR

Over the previous pages, we have seen three "paradoxes" of non-ergodicity.

1) It is not performance that is the most important factor for long-term performance but survival.

2) Something can work on average and still fail with permanent consequences.

3) What's best for the survival of the individual isn't necessarily what's best for the survival of the population, and the other way around.

All three assertions only apply to non-ergodic contexts. Hence the importance of understanding ergodicity. **Whether you are in an ergodic world or not determines what is rational and what isn't.**

Part 3
ERGODICITY

Here, you will find a definition of ergodicity and a few tests to determine whether a context is ergodic.

The last three parts of this book detail practical strategies to guide your actions in non-ergodic contexts.

CHAPTER 3.1
DEFINING ERGODICITY

A SIMPLE DEFINITION OF ERGODICITY[44]

A system [45] is ergodic if the lifetime outcome corresponds to the population outcome for all its components.

Otherwise, it is non-ergodic.

---

[44] As per the headline, this definition is incomplete. Here, I provided the simplest definition I could come with that applies to most practical cases, favoring clarity over precision. The next pages contain a more technical and precise definition.

[45] Or, more precisely, ergodicity is the property of a mathematical model describing a system. In particular, the adjective "ergodic" should refer to an observable in a mathematical model, as Ole Peters pointed out.

That said, for the sake of clarity, in this book, I will frequently use the adjective "non-ergodic" in relation to a system. This is because, in the examples I chose, it will be plausibly impossible to come out with a model representative of real life in which the system described is ergodic, at least in the context at hand.

PRACTICAL APPLICATIONS

Do not trust advice about a non-ergodic context that considers it ergodic.

Fully relying on averages and expected outcomes makes sense only in ergodic contexts. In non-ergodic ones, you want to ensure that you make decisions based on an estimate of your lifetime outcome.

When we see a behavior that we deem illogical or irrational, it is often worth asking ourselves, "is it irrational for an ergodic world, but rational for a non-ergodic one?"

A MORE TECHNICAL DEFINITION OF ERGODICITY

Here are a few, sometimes alternative, sometimes complementary, definitions of ergodicity.

Using the words of Ole Peters and Alexander Adamou,

> an observable [] is called ergodic if its expectation value is constant in time and its time average converges to this value with probability one
>
> (*Author's note: a reminder that expectation value and time average correspond to population and average outcome respectively.*)

Using the words of Frédéric Prost,

> ergodicity is verified if, more or less, every time that you compute a statistical measurement (across space or time), you find the same result. It means that randomness is "well shared." Another way to see it is that, when you have ergodicity, doing N random experiments in parallel will give you the same result as doing N experiments one after the other.

CHAPTER 3.2
ERGODICITY AND IRREVERSIBILITY

At the beginning of this book, we saw how skiing is non-ergodic. An injury causes a skier's championship to be over, nullifying any future win he could have collected in the remaining races. Similarly, it might cause his career to be over, nullifying any future earning he could have made.

We also saw how investing is non-ergodic. Bankruptcy is a form of game-over. It prevents you from collecting any possible future profit that your ventures might have made, had they survived.

Then, we saw how a healthcare system can work on average and still fail locally. This is because those who died do not resuscitate once a hospital works again. Death is a form of game-over: it nullifies any future gain.

Finally, we saw how public transportation is non-ergodic. You lose a flight when the train is late but do not gain a plane ticket when it arrives early. Again, being late could mean a form of game-over, and that brings non-ergodicity.

Game-overs bring non-ergodicity.

IRREVERSIBILITY

The previous page's concept can be generalized as follows. **Irreversibility brings non-ergodicity.**

After the game-over, you cannot keep playing. Game-overs are a form of irreversibility, but they are not the only one.

In some societies, once you're poor, you're likely to stay poor, and once you're rich, you're likely to stay rich. In these societies, one cannot assume that the lifetime outcome of a person born poor will coincide with the average of the population. He is likely to stay below average. Such a society in which wealth is at least partially irreversible is non-ergodic.

This is important because, for example, proactive redistribution is more relevant in societies such as the non-ergodic one described above than in those in which people already have ample social mobility.[46]

---

[46] All other things being equal, of course.

THE ERGODICITY TEST

Here is a simple test to spot non-ergodic situations. "Are there irreversible consequences?" If yes, it is non-ergodic.

This test is not complete. It doesn't identify all non-ergodic situations. However, a positive answer does imply that the situation at hand is non-ergodic.

In that case, you must avoid advice that does not take into account the sources of irreversibility.[47]

---

[47] Their technical name is absorption barriers.

CHAPTER 3.3
ERGODICITY AND EXPOSURE

There is a common misconception that ergodicity or non-ergodicity are properties of an activity. They are not. Take Russian Roulette, for example. It is non-ergodic for the gambler playing it but is rather ergodic for an imaginary company contracting gamblers to play Russian Roulette.[48] For this company, gamblers are replaceable. If enough time passes between rounds to have the time to recruit new gamblers to substitute dead ones, its lifetime outcome will match its population outcome.

Therefore, ergodicity is not just the property of an activity. Instead, **ergodicity is a property of an activity, its participants, and the exposure of the latter to the former** – in short, of a system.

---

[48] For the company, Russian Roulette is not fully ergodic, due to the small but nonzero possibility that most or all gamblers die at the same time, or that after a streak of bad luck, so many gamblers die that it goes bankrupt. Theoretically, ergodicity is a binary property. However, it's evident how "Russian Roulette is less non-ergodic when played by a company rather than a single gambler" is a meaningful statement. More on this in the chapter on the non-binary interpretation of ergodicity.

ERGODICITY – FOR INDIVIDUAL AND FOR SYSTEMS

Nassim Nicholas Taleb made a similar point. In his words, "My death at Russian roulette is not ergodic for me, but it is ergodic for the system." (This point will be further elaborated in the chapter on the Precautionary Principle.)

PRACTICAL IMPLICATIONS

The fact that ergodicity depends not only on the activity performed but also on your exposure to it is good news for you. It means that if you are careful about your exposure, you can still participate ergodically in non-ergodic activities. Or, that you can limit your exposure to non-ergodicity.

In the following chapter, you will learn in detail how to do it. Meanwhile, here are a few examples of methods that make you much less likely to hit a "game-over:"

- Instead of going all-in on a single bet, take many independent bets.[49]

- Use protections (of all kinds – Personal Protective Equipment, insurances, capped-downside options, and so on).

- Set aside some buffers and reserves (of money, time, trust, etc.) so that even if you lose everything you used, you still have some to recover.

---

[49] Make sure that they are really independent, though! A real-estate investor is not really diversifying by purchasing two buildings in the same city. Or, to be more precise, he is diversifying against some risks (e.g., an explosion from a gas leak) but not against others (e.g., the city losing jobs).

CHAPTER 3.4
ERGODICITY AS A NON-BINARY PROPERTY

Formally, ergodicity is a binary property. A system is either ergodic or not. The lifetime outcomes of its participants coincide with its population outcome, or they don't – nothing in between.

In theory, this is a useful distinction. If you can choose between acting in an ergodic or non-ergodic context, choose the former, or be extremely careful.

In practice, however, most practical contexts are non-ergodic. Work, sports, relationships, and real life are all non-ergodic. They all contain some degree of irreversibility.

It becomes then useful to expand the concept of ergodicity from black and white to a scale of shades. This way, we can access more practical considerations such as "how can I make my business more ergodic?"

In the example from the previous page, a company hiring Russian Roulette players is not a truly ergodic activity. There are still points of irreversibility. For example, some bad luck in which all gamblers die might bankrupt the company. However, for all practical purposes, the assertion "Russian Roulette is more ergodic if played by a company contracting gamblers rather than by a single gambler" makes a lot of sense.[50]

Yes, the lifetime outcome of both tends to zero at infinite time. However, in real life, there is no such thing as infinite time. In any plausible finite time, the company's lifetime outcome is likely to be close to its population outcome. Conversely, the outcomes of players differ. Hence the justification for expressions such as "more ergodic" or "less ergodic."

---

[50] It means that, *in the medium term,* the lifetime outcome is closer to that of its population for a company than for a single player.

ERGODICITY AND DECISION-MAKING

On the one hand, only the fools optimize for the short-term. On the other hand, few people make decisions aiming at maximizing the long-term, here intended as more than a few decades. This would only be optimal if they could predict how they and the world will change (new circumstances mean that what was optimal is now suboptimal). Instead, most people set for themselves medium-term goals, such as saving enough money to buy a house, reaching a managerial position, or marrying.

Therefore, if you studied ergodicity to increase your chances of achieving your goals or to understand human behavior, a black-and-white definition of ergodicity that considers infinite timeframes does little good. **It is more effective to study ergodicity on medium-term timeframes.**

Most people do not care if an activity has a source of irreversibility. Instead, they care whether irreversibility has a non-negligible chance of manifesting within the period they see themselves performing the activity. In other words, what matters is not whether the lifetime and the population outcomes diverge over infinite time-frames – what matters is if they do noticeably over the medium term.

Moreover, as pointed out before, people cannot realistically avoid any non-ergodic activity. We all need to perform many of them in our lives. Therefore, people do not only care whether an activity is non-ergodic; they care how much it is.

Hence, **for most people, what matters is** *how much* the lifetime outcome diverges from the population outcome *in the medium term.*

This is the justification and definition for my use, within this book, of a non-binary interpretation of ergodicity.

THE IRREVERSIBILITY OF TIME

In most of the examples described so far, non-ergodicity caused a permanent loss of money, health, reputation, or other assets. There is one more resource that we lose permanently: time.

No calculation, thought experiment, or study can pretend to model real-life behavior if it assumes time as infinite. Such an arbitrary and unwarranted assumption can lead to mistakenly classify an irrational behavior as rational or the other way around.

CHAPTER 3.5
IN SEARCH OF ERGODICITY

In the book so far, we have seen the problem with non-ergodicity: it causes your lifetime outcome to be worse than the expected one.

In many situations, you want to increase the ergodicity of the systems you're a part of. For example, if you are an investor, the less ergodic are your investments, the less their lifetime returns.[51] Hence, you want to make your investments as ergodic as possible.[52] Similarly, if you are the manager of an organization, you want to increase its ergodicity – so that a downturn doesn't make it go out of business. The same applies if you are a freelancer.

The rest of this book acknowledges this need. It presents you with three strategies that you can use to make a system more ergodic.[53]

---

[51] All other things being equal.

[52] Here, and for the rest of the book, I refer to (non)ergodicity as a non-binary property. The motivations have been explained in the previous pages.

[53] Some readers might have recognized that there are situations in which you want to prevent something from surviving. For example, cancer, or zombie companies in a bull market. This is still about increasing ergodicity – at the higher layer. For example, introducing irreversibility so that zombie companies go bankrupt decreases the ergodicity of companies but increases the ergodicity of the market. This relationship between survival at different layers is explored more in detail in my 2018 book "The Power Of Adaptation."

Part 4
REDUCING EXPOSURE

One source of non-ergodicity is irrecoverable situations, or "game-overs." For example, bankruptcy, death, social ostracization, and permanent injuries. It is natural, then, that the first of the three strategies to manage non-ergodicity is to reduce exposure to game-over.

The simplest and surest way to do so is to refuse to participate in any activity that has such a risk. Duh.

This works great in theory. However, in real life, we can seldomly adopt such a strategy. We cannot decide not to leave our house for fear of incidents. Nor can we keep all our money in a safe – if we did, inflation would erode our wealth.

In real life, two better options are what Nassim Nicholas Taleb calls a Barbell strategy and the Kelly Criterion – the topics of the next two chapters.

CHAPTER 4.1
THE BARBELL STRATEGY

The barbell is a gym equipment in which most of the weight is at the sides, and there is a long stick in between. It is more effective than a regular rod of the same weight.

In investing, the barbell strategy consists of allocating part of one's wealth in non-risky assets and part in risky ones with high upside (the asymmetry being reminiscent of a barbell). Investors who do so find themselves wealthier than those investing all their wealth in medium-risk assets[54] (a shape that would remind of a regular rod). One of the reasons is a medium-risk investment is less likely to suffer large *losses but is not immune to them.* And, over long-enough timeframes, "less likely" means "eventually."

---

[54] Over the long-term. Counterexamples are prone to survivorship bias. When measuring this effect, we shall be wary of considering the same cohort over the long term, not the whole market full of new entrants.

The barbell strategy consists of exposing most of yourself to safe activities and a tiny bit of yourself to risky ones with high upside.

This is distinct from exposing all of yourself to safe activities[55] most of the time and seldomly to risky ones with high upside. Doing so puts you at risk of game-over while you perform the latter. Conversely, **the point of the barbell strategy is to pursue risky activities in a way that caps downside.**

The barbell strategy extends beyond investing. In business, it means to allocate most of your time to activities with safe returns and just a bit in risky ventures whose success can be life-changing. In life, it means to secure your bases and take small limited-downside high-upside bets.

This apparently banal strategy is clever than it seems. **By reducing the amount exposed to risk, it prevents a single loss, or a short series of losses, from constituting a game-over.** It also gives you the opportunity, after some bad luck, to "exit" – a luxury that more invested participants lack.

Moreover, this strategy acknowledges that, **in most contexts, a small exposure to high upside brings higher returns than a moderate exposure to moderate upside.** This is particularly relevant in contexts where returns cluster. That said, the distribution of returns is not the point here. What matters is that you can afford small risky bets for longer. Otherwise, if you lose a few moderate bets with moderate upside, you're done.

---

[55] In this context, "safe activity" = limited downside, low upside.

THE BARBELL STRATEGY AND ERGODICITY

One lesson from Taleb's work is that **risk management is not about prudence but about removing the risks of "game-over" so that you can be aggressive with other risks.**

Similarly, **the barbell strategy is not about reducing risk in general. Instead, it is about limiting the part of yourself or of your assets that are exposed to irreversibility.**

A balanced or medium-risk exposure does not do the trick. It would be like playing Russian Roulette with one-in-twelve bullets rather than one-in-six: it just means that the game-over is delayed but does not prevent it. Conversely, the barbell strategy is like playing Russian Roulette without pointing the gun to your skull but to a $100 banknote. If you're unlucky (*when* you're unlucky), you only lose the banknote, not your life.

Accordingly, here is an alternative formulation of the barbell strategy. "Preserve your ergodicity by investing in non-ergodic activities only what can be lost without endangering the whole."

APPLYING THE BARBELL STRATEGY

As a professional, I apply the barbell strategy by always looking for new business opportunities but never entering any in such a full and decisive manner that its failure could endanger my livelihood.

I also apply the barbell strategy with my investments, allocating most of my money to safe "ergodic assets" and taking small speculative bets with the rest.

More in general, I look for risk but make sure that I never approach it in such a way that an unexpected event might irreversibly affect my life in any significant matter.

ERGODICITY IS NOT FREE[56]

Ergodicity helps us survive and thus grab eventual future gains but also comes with opportunity costs. If you limit your exposure to risk, you often limit your exposure to upsides too. For example, if you limit your investment portfolio exposure to stocks, you also limit your gains from an eventual bull market and thus expose yourself to other negative events.[57]

That's okay. Hopefully, this book gave you the tools to justify to yourself and others that the long-term benefits of avoiding game-overs are well worth the opportunity costs.

---

[56] I first read this expression from Italian trader Stefano Peron.

[57] Stefano Peron also makes the point that ergodicity over a risk might increase other risks. For example, a trader with a limited stock exposure might get fired by his boss during a bull market, for his returns are temporarily subpar.

A SUMMARY OF THE FIRST STRATEGY

The Barbell strategy is about limiting exposure so that the worst-case scenario doesn't endanger your survival. It makes the non-ergodic ergodic, for most practical purposes.

In practice, it consists of investing a large part of yourself in limited-downside activities and a small part in high-upside ones. In particular, an activity with a tiny chance of a ruinous outcome is *not* considered "limited-downside."

CHAPTER 4.2
THE KELLY CRITERION

Let's imagine that you're playing the following gambling game. You have $100. Your ten best friends attempt to shoot a ball into a basket. Before each shoots, you decide how much to bet on his shot going in. If they make it, you double your bet. If they fail, you lose it. What's the best strategy to maximize your gains?

You might have had the following two intuitions. First, you do not want to bet all your money on a single shot. If your friend misses, you lose all your money. You cannot make further bets and thus cannot benefit from eventual wins you could have had in the future. That was the lesson of Russian Roulette: losses absorb future gains.

Second, you want to bet more on your friends who are good at basketball and less on those who are being clumsier.

These two intuitions, "don't go all-in" and "payoffs determine the relative size of the bet," summarize a betting strategy known as the Kelly Criterion, named after the mathematician who invented it. I won't cover the exact formula, for this book aims to build an intuitive understanding of ergodicity, not a mathematical one. What matters is **that risk exposure must depend on payoffs and, anyway, be limited.**

HOW I APPLIED THE KELLY CRITERION TO MY LIFE

I routinely use the Kelly Criterion[58]. As an author, consultant, and researcher, I spend most of my time writing books and essays, working with clients, and researching. All of these projects take time, and time is money. If I invested all my time for the next three years on a single project or client, I would be in a terrible condition in case of failure. Instead, I allocate my time on a per-project basis. Usually, the larger the upside, the more time I spend on the project. However, I always make sure to never commit all of my time to a single project running for extended time. Too much to lose, both in case the project doesn't go well or in terms of opportunity costs.

---

[58] Formally, $f^* = [\, p\,(b+1) - 1\,]\,/\,b$

Where f* is the fraction of the current bankroll to wager; (i.e. how much to bet, expressed in fraction),

b is the net fractional odds received on the wager.

E.g. if on a $10 the win is $4 plus the wager, then $b = 0.4$.

p is the probability of a win.

CHAPTER 4.3
THE KELLY CRITERION IN NATURE

I find it fascinating that some animals, including us humans, have two psychological processes that, together, approximate the Kelly Criterion.[59] They are moods and fears. The following two pages describe them.

---

[59] I do not intend that moods and fears fully reproduce the Kelly criterion, not that they alone approximate it – just, that they help approximating it, within the range of what is reasonably possible to do with instincts alone.

MOODS AND THE KELLY CRITERION

In our society, many see being moody as a problem. This is true to some extent, but moods are generally beneficial. For example, consider two hunter-gatherers, Alice and Bob. They live in a territory where the main source of food is berries growing under bushes. Some bushes have no berries, whereas others are full of them. Gathering them is a tiring activity, for one has to walk close to a bush and lift some of its leaves to know whether it contains any berry. Bob is moody, whereas Alice cannot feel any mood. Who do you think is a better gatherer, all other things being equal?

The answer is Bob. He is more likely to check the bushes with berries and not check those without berries. How come?

Well, Alice does not feel any mood, so she would tend to sample every bush she walks by – an inefficient method. Instead, Bob would check the first bush, then the second one, then he might become discouraged (a mood), and he would walk for a bit before bending forward to check the bush next to him. Once he finds some berries, he gets excited (another mood) and checks all the bushes nearby. This is advantageous because, in nature, resources tend to cluster together. If a bush is particularly fruitful, the chances are that the ones around it are too, because they grow on the same fertile soil.

Moods are tools to adapt to environments with clustered resources.

As the hunter-gatherers' example showed, **moderately moody people tend to be more efficient than moodless ones.** (The keyword being "moderately" – excesses are bad.)

This theory[60] of moods is interesting. It shows how moods improve effectiveness by making people spend more time on what looks promising and less time on what is likely to be a waste of time. Moreover, they reduce exposition to what is dangerous (wasting time and energy), thereby improving survival. They allow us to adapt much more precisely to a world where threats and resources are not uniformly distributed. A must, in a non-ergodic world.

In particular, you might have noticed a similarity with the Kelly Criterion. Moods cause us to intuitively bet more time and energy on activities with high payoffs and less on activities with low payoffs.

---

[60] Influenced by "Mood as Representation of Momentum", Eldar E., Rutledge R. B., Dolan R. J., and Niv Y., 2016.

A PRACTICAL EXAMPLE FROM MY LIFE

A few pages ago, I mentioned how I allocate my time to my projects by informally following the Kelly Criterion. However, I didn't tell you that my decision on how much time to allocate to a project is rarely deliberate. Rather, it is based on moods such as excitement. As I begin exploring a project, if I find early successes or interesting bits, my excitement grows, and so does the share of my time I decide to allocate to the project. In the end, the result is similar to what I would have obtained had I applied the Kelly Criterion formally.

FEAR AND THE KELLY CRITERION

Moods alone would not be enough to approximate the Kelly Criterion, though. Modulating bets based on payoffs is only one of its two components. The other is to avoid going all-in. Fear is an adaptation that helps us with that.

If we didn't feel fear, a few successes in a row would cause us to be in an ecstatic mood and go all-in. Fear helps us maintaining some prudence.

Similarly, a few failures in a row might cause us to abandon any will to do anything. Fear of missing out, fear of starvation, fear of being labeled as lazy, and similar fears keep us at least somehow motivated and active.

Fear helps counterbalancing moods. Together, they work a bit like the Kelly Criterion, allowing us to adapt to a non-ergodic world.

MOODS AND FEARS ARE NOT JUST ABOUT SURVIVAL

There are mathematical demonstrations that the Kelly Criterion is a very effective strategy not only for survival but also for wealth maximization. This means that *moderately* moody and fearful people not only avoid dangers but also accumulate more wealth and other resources.

Of course, this only applies to moderately moody and fearful people, not to excessively moody and fearful ones. Excesses are not good. If they seem so, you must be entertaining a narrow definition of success. Sadly, many artifacts of our modern times, such as sugar-rich foods and gambling, are designed to induce excesses.

THE CURSE OF MODERNITY

I learned on my skin that moods and fears are sometimes fallible. For example, I remember the first time I ate ice-cream from a box, as a kid. I couldn't stop myself. If it weren't for the box being finite, I would have gone into sugar overdose. Similarly, I remember the traumatic experience I had the first time our elementary school brought us to swim. Afterward, I didn't want to immerse myself in water for a few months. Sometimes, moods and fears lead to excesses, such as addictions and trauma.

Moods and fears analyze whether a given situation is auspicious or ominous. As with any categorization tool, they are prone to false positives and false negatives. Natural selection caused our brain to adapt to the optimal tradeoff. However, as with any trade-off, optimal doesn't mean perfect.

I have noticed that this particularly applies to modern activities that didn't exist in the past – such as eating ice-cream. Our moods and fears adapted to the environment our ancestors evolved in, not to the modern environment in which you and I live. In particular, moods and fears become liabilities when we are exposed to artifacts of the modern world designed to take advantage of them – again, such as ice-cream.

That said, even though they are sometimes wrong, moods and fears are still important assets. They are not perfect by any means, but we are better off with them than without.

A SUMMARY SO FAR

We saw that non-ergodicity is a dangerous condition. You want to make sure you know what you are doing.

The first strategy to apply is to make sure that you never go all-in in any activity that might represent a game-over for you in case of misfortune.

As seen in the Barbell strategy, this is distinct from never taking any risks. Just take them with a limited exposure – for example, by investing just a little. The Kelly Criterion helped you understand how to modulate your bets better.

In the next chapter, we will see how the concepts described above apply not only to our actions but also to our society's.[61]

---

[61] I try as much as possible, in this book and in other ventures, to frequently zoom in and out across scales. This is an encouraged behavior, for you might discover that what works at one scale might not work at another. Or, you might discover that you have in your hands a principle that applies at any scale. Either way, you don't know until you try.

CHAPTER 4.4
THE PRECAUTIONARY PRINCIPLE

The Precautionary Principle guides us in risk management decisions. It begins by acknowledging that there are two kinds of risks: those that endanger the whole (a population, an ecosystem, the planet) and those that do not.

For example, if someone drives too fast and crashes, he might die, and he might also kill a few people, but the population in general is not affected. This is an example of a risk that can kill an individual without endangering the whole. These risks are safe to take for the population. In some cases, they even make it stronger.

Conversely, some risks have the potential to destroy the whole population. We should avoid these risks at all costs.

The Precautionary Principle holds that we should not take risks that endanger the whole, no matter how unlikely. If we keep taking them, we are guaranteed to blow up (remember the Russian Roulette player?).

When they hear about the Precautionary Principle, some reply, "So what, we never do anything?" This response is wrong, as the next page shows.

THE PRECAUTIONARY PRINCIPLE IS NOT ABOUT FULL PRUDENCE

The Precautionary Principle does not say to avoid all risks – just those that can destroy the whole. In the words of Nassim Nicholas Taleb, who authored a homonymous paper[62]: "My death at Russian roulette is not ergodic for me, but it is ergodic for the system. The precautionary principle, in the formulation I did with a few colleagues, is precisely about the highest layer [the system]."

In other words, feel free to play Russian Roulette by pointing the gun at your skull, but do not play it by pointing the gun at the ecosystem.

Nuclear power plants are an example of a risk that, while scary, is contained.
No explosion, no matter how deadly to its surroundings, can endanger the planet.

---

[62] The Precautionary Principle (with Application to the Genetic Modification of Organisms), Nassim Nicholas Taleb, Rupert Read, Raphael Douady, Joseph Norman, Yaneer Bar-Yam, 2014.

The Precautionary Principle only applies to risks that endanger the whole, not risks that only endanger the local. An example of the latter is nuclear plants – if one blows up, it destroys its surroundings, but not the planet. Moreover, a disaster makes other plants less likely to blow up, as we learn about failure points and establish new safety procedures. Instead, the Precautionary Principle applies to risks that can potentially destroy the human race or the ecosystem.[63]

---

[63] An example: GMOs.

Genetically modified organisms, "GMOs" in short, are plants and animals that scientists genetically modified to bestow them some desirable properties, such as parasite resistance. They are a potential source of good. Some say that they could eradicate malaria or hunger. Sadly, they are also a potential source of harm. For example, it is possible that we create some GMO mosquitoes to fight malaria, and some unexpected interaction causes the initiative to backfire.

Any new technology has a chance of backfiring. However, when they do, most technologies backfire locally. For example, when a nuclear plant explodes, it "only" harms the surrounding territory. Other nuclear plants can be shut down, and the situation can be quickly reassessed, as it happened after the terrible Chernobyl incident in 1986.

Conversely, we would have a hard time stopping a GMO that is found harmful after its broad introduction in the ecosystem. Good luck catching GMO mosquitoes.

Hence, GMOs are risky in a way that nuclear plants aren't. Only the former have the potential to destroy the ecosystem.

Note: GMOs didn't create any systemic problem so far. This doesn't exclude that they won't produce any in the future. We just began experimenting with them. Therefore, to estimate their risks, we shall study not the past but the properties of their possible interactions with the ecosystem.

RISK OF RUIN AND COST-BENEFIT ANALYSES

We saw how we can classify risks into two categories: those with the *potential* to kill the ecosystem and those without.

Here comes the critical bit. **We cannot use cost-benefit analysis with risks that can kill the ecosystem. If we take enough risks of this type with a positive cost-benefit analysis, we are guaranteed to kill the ecosystem.**

In the first chapter of this book, we saw how the expected returns of playing the Russian Roulette decrease with the number of times it is played by the same gambler (see the chart below).

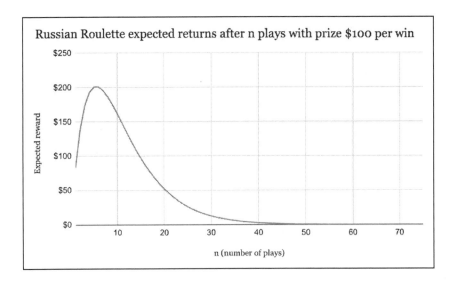

The lesson is: **do not expose the whole to irreversibility, no matter how attractive the payoffs.**

For example, an epidemic so deadly that it endangers the human species is a possible systemic risk. Until we have a foolproof demonstration that no virus, no matter how deadly, can endanger the human race, we should take precautions, no matter how costly.

The most common argument against precautions is that they are expensive. This is not a valid argument. Payoffs are subordinate to ergodicity, so we cannot use them until we can be sure that epidemics are not a systemic risk.

You cannot compare apple to oranges, nor systemic risks to local ones. The only valid argument in contradiction of a precaution against a systemic risk could be that the precaution itself introduces a similar or larger systemic risk. (That said, hopefully, the 2020 pandemic showed us the costs of no prevention.)

CHAPTER 4.5
NATURAL SELECTION AND FRACTALIZATION

Natural selection is usually is a scary process, threatening our livelihoods. However, it is possible to make it work for us rather than against us. In this chapter, I will show you how to harness the power of natural selection.

MULTISCALE NATURAL SELECTION

In nature, those who are fit thrive, and the unfit perish. Natural selection is a cruel yet essential phenomenon. Without it, we humans would perhaps not exist, nor civilization as we know it.

Natural selection also takes place in business. The best companies expand, open new stores, and launch more products. The worst ones fall into bankruptcy.[64]

The same phenomenon applies to the components of companies: employees. The best ones climb in rank. The worst ones get fired.

---

[64] Free markets are petri dishes where experiments are continuously performed (new ventures), the survivors decided by what works, not by what makes sense – this is the true engine of innovation.

An organization that never fires a single employee becomes uncompetitive. Natural selection at the level of the industry will make the company fail. Therefore, to avoid becoming a victim of natural selection, a company must make it act on its employees, at least in a measure.

Natural selection is inevitable for companies, but they can decide whether it acts on them or within them (in a measure).

However, firing employees is not that good either. It has heavy consequences, especially on the fired employee and his or her family. It is something that we want to avoid within reason.

The solution is to realize that **natural selection, while inevitable, can be further pushed down to lower levels.** Just like companies can protect themselves by firing their unfit employees, employees can protect themselves by firing their unfit mental patterns.

To protect the individual, natural selection must be free to act within the individual. There, it can select the beliefs and habits of his or hers that are fit (i.e., beneficial) and terminate those that are unfit (i.e., hinder his or her performance).

FRACTALIZATION

I call the process described above *fractalization*. The name comes from the realization that natural selection acts across levels with a fractal-like pattern.[65] Just as it acts within a market by selecting companies, it acts within companies selecting employees, within individuals selecting beliefs, and within beliefs selecting fragments.

I mean it in the broadest sense possible. For example, species are made of individuals, and individuals of muscle fibers. By exercising, and thus breaking one's muscle fibers, one gets stronger and reduces his chances (and that of his population) of becoming the victim of natural selection. Similarly, markets are made of businesses, businesses of employees, and employees of beliefs and habits.[66]

Each level can protect itself from natural selection by becoming stronger. That requires letting natural selection working within itself. **Natural selection is inevitable, but we can avoid it at any given level by pushing it towards a lower one** (in some measure).

---

[65] "Fractal-like," not "fractal." I know well that the latter has a very restrictive meaning. Yet, I use here the terms "fractal-like" and "fractalization" as I found them very effective to convey an intuitive understanding of the phenomenon described in this chapter. As mentioned in the introduction, in the inevitable tradeoff between clarity and precision, I here favored clarity.

[66] I arrived at this conclusion while thinking about the antifragile (a concept described in Nassim Nicholas Taleb's homonymous book). One of the three requirements for an entity to be antifragile is for it to comprise elements that can be independently damaged. From there, I realized that taking the monolithic and making it a multitude is a major step towards antifragility.

You, too, can take advantage of natural selection. Remember: whenever it encounters a population, it "kills" some of its members. Therefore, you can become stronger by making yourself a population – of habits and beliefs – and getting rid of the unfit ones. Even though your ego wants to save them.

People that consider their identity one and indivisible prevent natural selection from acting *within* them. Therefore, they do not grow stronger. Instead, they become vulnerable to natural selection acting *on* them.

If you want to survive, do not identify with your habits and beliefs but with their container. This way, you will let natural selection remove the habits and beliefs that are holding you down. You will get stronger, thus less likely to become the victim of natural selection yourself.

(An additional point, from Nassim Nicholas Taleb. "As I have shown in Antifragile, the fragility of the components is required to ensure the solidity of the system. If humans were immortals, they would go extinct from an accident or a gradual buildup of misfitness. But shorter shelf life for humans allows genetic changes to accompany the variability in the environment.")

EXAMPLE OF A PRACTICAL APPLICATION

As a teenager, I was shy. I had a lot of friends, but I would seldom ask girls out. If I did, I would do so in such an awkward way that they would refuse my invitation.

If my shyness continued, I could see myself becoming a victim of natural selection. I would end up alone and childless. Thankfully, I realized that the problem wasn't myself but my shyness. In particular, the problem was the mental beliefs of mine that made me shy with girls.

Once I realized that they were the problem, I could get rid of them.[67] I am now a confident man.

---

[67] We are extremely good at getting rid of the beliefs that we acknowledge being the source of our problems, *once we realize that there is no alternative.* Usually, this happens when we try everything else and still fail. Until then, getting rids of the mental patterns that are holding us back will be hard – rather than doing that, we look for alternatives. Instead of removing, we add. Often, the opposite is better.

CHAPTER 4.6
SUMMARY OF THE FIRST STRATEGY, REDUCING EXPOSURE

The first strategy to manage non-ergodicity is to reduce your exposure to irreversibility. In particular, we saw how:

- **You can only optimize in reversible domains.** Otherwise, you should think about avoiding irreversibility.

- **You can reduce exposure to irreversibility by exposing only part of yourself** (or of your assets, or reputation, etc.). This is safer and more effective than going all-in on a medium-risk activity.

- **It is safer to keep a bit of yourself exposed to risk** (to grab some upside) than not doing it. Otherwise, we involuntarily expose ourselves to the risks of inaction and obsolescence.

- An effective tactic is to **design systems as fractals** and decrease the ergodicity of the lower layers to increase that of the higher ones.

- **Nature gave us tools to manage non-ergodicity, in the form of moods and fear.**

Here are a few ways in which you can apply the first strategy:

- **Invest your money as a barbell** (most in low-downside assets, a bit in high-upside ones).

- **Invest your time as a barbell** (most in activities that make your bedrock stronger, a bit in explorative ones).

- **Purposefully test your habits and beliefs** to get rid of those that are negatively impacting your life or making you weak.

THE PATH FORWARD

The next chapter is about the second strategy to manage non-ergodicity: skin in the game.

Part 5

ENSURE THAT THE DANGEROUS GETS REMOVED

My favorite book of 2018 is Nassim Nicholas Taleb's *Skin In The Game*.

My baker has skin in the game. If his bread is bad, he loses reputation and clients. He might have to close his shop, eventually. In general, **someone has skin in the game if, when wrong, he becomes the victim of his mistakes.**

Conversely, some managers can squeeze their team, take short-term decisions with catastrophic consequences, and then leave to another team or company without suffering from the long-term consequences of their actions. They do not have skin in the game.

Skin in the game is of paramount importance because it protects populations and individuals. It does so in three ways. The following chapters describe them one by one.

CHAPTER 5.1
SKIN IN THE GAME REDUCES THE MORAL HAZARD

Decision-makers who can take short-termed decisions without being affected by their long-term consequences take excessive risks. This condition is called *moral hazard.*

Moral hazard happens when someone has incentives to increase an entity's exposure to risk because he won't bear the full cost of that risk.

Other examples of moral hazards are parents imposing stressful career choices on their kids, bigots forbidding protected sex, and unethical doctors suggesting unnecessary medical procedures.

The condition of suffering the consequences of one's actions, **"skin in the game," is the opposite of moral hazard.** It incentivizes people to make decisions that are good for them *and* others. As such, **it helps protecting populations.**

However, incentivization is not the only way skin in the game protects from harm. The next page shows another one.

CHAPTER 5.2

SKIN IN THE GAME REMOVES SOURCES OF IRREVERSIBILITY

Speeding fines incentivize drivers not to exceed speed limits. And yet, some drivers keep going too fast and collecting fines. Part of the reason is that, for some drivers, fines are like fees. They are a cost that might be worth paying.[68]

A single speeding fine does not prevent the driver from driving again. If it were only for fines, drivers would be incentivized not to go fast, but would not have skin in the game.

---

[68] As a rule of thumb, we tend to neglect incentives that do not hit a bottleneck.

Conversely, crashing is an event that can stop a driver from driving again – either because he died or because the police canceled his driving license. **It is not incentives that provide skin in the game, but irreversibility.**[69,70]

IRREVERSIBILITY, FOR WHOM?

Irreversibility is not always bad. In a previous chapter, we saw that when we talk about irreversibility, we must specify the layer at which it takes place.

A dangerous criminal ending up in prison is bad for him but good for the upper layer: society. Similarly, a corrupt politician getting exposed and banned from public office is bad for him but good for society.

Populations want their members to have skin in the game. This way, over time, they get rid of those that expose themselves and others to risks.

---

[69] In his book, Taleb makes the point that skin in the game is not about incentives but filtering.

[70] Some countries have a points-based driving license system, in which drivers lose points every time they break a law. This works fairly well but only partially counts as skin in the game, as not all drivers who drive dangerously are caught (and of those who do, in some countries, some can escape the penalty by declaring they weren't the ones at the wheel and paying a higher fine).

POPULATIONS, ERGODICITY, & SKIN IN THE GAME

As we saw two pages ago, skin in the game requires irreversibility. Incentives that can be part of a cost-benefit analysis are not enough. A dangerous player might neglect them, whereas no one can neglect irreversibility.

And, as we saw on the last page, one member abandoning a population due to skin in the game benefits the population.

A population can decrease its exposure to irreversibility by exposing its members to it. Whether irreversibility has a positive or negative effect depends on the layer observed.

LIMITATIONS

Of course, this is only valid for exposures to irreversibility that do not have the potential to destroy a sizeable chunk of the population. Reckless drivers dying in car crashes do make cities safer[71], for they disappear before they can hurt too many people, but inventors dying from creating an atomic bomb in their garage do not (though they probably do make the world safer by raising a concern and triggering a response to it – again, it depends from the layer making the observation).

---

[71] Given that dangerous drivers exist, we are better off with them disappearing soon rather than later. Yes, we would be better off if dangerous drivers didn't even begin driving, but that's not realistic, not with the current transportation system.

SUMMARY OF THIS CHAPTER

Skin in the game prevents dangerous individuals from hurting others. It does so in two ways. First, it incentivizes them not to do anything dangerous. Second, if they do, it prevents them from doing it again.

CHAPTER 5.3
SKIN IN THE GAME PREVENTS DANGEROUS BEHAVIORS FROM SPREADING

In the previous chapter, we saw how skin in the game prevents dangerous individuals from putting others in danger. This is not the only way skin in the game makes a population safer.

Take the example of frauds and charlatans. Most populations contain a few. In the absence of skin in the game, they can perpetuate their scam without consequences. They become famous. People imitate them instead of someone more competent. As a result, ineffective or dangerous behaviors spread. This is bad.

Conversely, in the presence of skin in the game, the success of charlatans is short-lived. Their mistakes cause them to leave the pool of celebrities people imitate before they influence the behavior of too many.

Skin in the game prevents dangerous or ineffective behaviors from spreading. It ensures that frauds, charlatans, and incompetents are quickly filtered out of the pool of experts that people imitate.

Additional notes: ergodicity and digital culture [72]*, the importance of immediacy for skin in the game*[73]*, and mimetic societies*[74]*.*

---

[72] In his essay "Ergodicity And Digital Culture," Frédéric Prost makes the following point (here, paraphrased or quoted). In oral tradition, information spreads slowly, by word of mouth, from its practitioners. Information is filtered through time. Therefore, the behaviors that spread tend to be those that help with survival. In written tradition, information is filtered through the elites and the editors. [The information that survives tends to help with their survival.] Conversely, in "internet tradition," spreading information is cheap and can be done instantaneously and by people without skin in the game. As a result, dangerous behaviors can easily spread wide. Culture building is non ergodic, for its spread through time yields different results than its spread through populations and digital culture achieves different results than oral tradition.

[73] As an example, contrary to common belief, many CEOs in the US and in many other countries do not appear to have skin in the game. Not in the short- and medium-term, at least – their violations and their companies' go unpunished or yield fines that are similar to fees for bad behavior rather than limitations to conduct harmful business. This lack of *effective immediate* skin in the game coupled with their celebrity means that they become an attractive model whose behaviors to copy.

It is possible that these CEOs get criminally convicted at some point in the future. That doesn't matter, for the purpose of behavioral imitation. **If skin in the game materializes much more slowly than behaviors spreads, it is *as if* there were none.**

What matters is not theoretical skin in the game. All entrepreneurs have it. Instead, what matters is if dangerous behaviors actually result in the entrepreneur losing his business or hitting some other form of game-over. If that doesn't happen, **or happens too slowly,** then the dangerous behavior spreads well before its consequences materialize. It's *as if* there wasn't skin in the game, for the practical purposes at hand.

[74] "Mimetic societies" is a short essay of mine freely available at bit.ly/mimeticsocieties

CHAPTER 5.4
SUMMARY OF THE SECOND STRATEGY, SKIN IN THE GAME

We saw how:

- **Skin in the game acts as an incentive *and* as a filter** that removes dangerous individuals from the community and prevents dangerous behaviors from spreading.

- **Sociality helps aligning incentives within a community** and conserving precious variance. It makes one feel like he cannot act against his community and then "jump ships."

Here are some practical applications:

- **Be wary of advice from people without skin in the game.**

- **Be wary of envying people without skin in the game.** Imitating them might expose you to problems you didn't consider.

- **Careful of removing social bonding from your life or organization in the name of efficiency:** it has a purpose.

Part 6

REDISTRIBUTION

In the second part of this book, we saw how Italian hospitals didn't get very busy with COVID *on average*, yet some got overwhelmed. **Systems can function well on average and yet fail locally.**

If the overwhelmed hospitals in Northern Italy could have instantaneously transferred the patients to the less busy ones of other regions, there would have been no difference between the local and the average. Each hospital would have been just as busy as any other one.

However, in reality, hospitals cannot redistribute their patients fast enough. Hence, the local failures.

An important factor that influences whether a system working well on average also works well everywhere is redistribution.

The question that we must ask ourselves is, "When there is a local spike in load, can the system redistribute the load fast enough?"[75]

---

[75] A system that can redistribute load quickly is not immune to failure, just much less likely.

For example, a system that can perfectly redistribute growth will break once the load exceeds the number of load-bearing units times the unit's load capacity. The slower is the system in redistributing, the lower will be the maximum load it can withstand.

This part of the book explains how redistribution help managing non-ergodicity. The next chapter is about load redistribution, and the following one about financial redistribution. You will learn how redistribution can help you, even when you're already the best.

...

An example: bulletproof jackets work by dispersing the load from the bullet hitting them across a large surface.

If the hit load were restricted to a small area, it would pierce the clothing.

CHAPTER 6.1
LOAD REDISTRIBUTION

In the previous pages, we saw how hospitals would not have trouble managing local surges in hospitalization if they could instantaneously redistribute patients across all hospitals.

Systems that can instantaneously share load are more ergodic than those that cannot, all other things equal. For them, the local and the average are the same.[76]

This phenomenon applies to countries and large organizations, but also individuals. For example, the waiting room at my doctor's was frequently overcrowded. He knew he had to do something. The expensive solution was to rent a larger studio with a larger waiting room. The smart solution was to take telephonic booking. A booking system helps to redistribute loads (in this case, patients) over time.

This is important. Spikes in load can cause irreversibility: patients changing doctors because of too long waiting time (forever lost customers) and patients getting illnesses from staying too long in a crowded waiting room.

---

[76] At least on the dimension of the particular load at hand.

As another example, a good friend of mine recently purchased a car. He chose to pay it in monthly installments over five years. He did so even though he had the financial availability to pay it cash. He explained that it allowed him to keep a buffer of money in the bank, to manage unexpected problems. If he paid the car cash and lost his job next month, he would be in dire straits.

This makes sense! He decided to prioritize survival over optimization, the unexpected over the expected. Conversely, a clueless economist might call irrational the choice to pay something more, when you have the option to pay it less. Temporal distribution matters.

Similarly, I've recently learned to appreciate actions that seem inefficient but increase my resilience to sudden spikes in load. For example, in the past, I tried to schedule all meetings in the city center on the same weekday. This way, I would only have to travel there once. Now, I try to spread them over two days. Yes, it means that I must commute twice. But it also allows me to benefit from unexpected events that would otherwise destroy my schedule, such as a client asking me to stay longer or a friend unexpectedly inviting me for lunch.

Pre-emptive redistribution increases resilience and opens up opportunities.

POST-MORTEMS AND PRE-MORTEMS

In large organizations, when a project ends, it is common to do a *post-mortem* (it means "after-death"). It is a meeting in which the project manager and his team meet and ask themselves, "What did go wrong? What should we do differently next time?"

Post-mortems bring precious insights. They are a useful practice. Even more useful are *pre-mortems*. These are meetings held at the beginning of a project, in which the team asks, "Let's imagine that the project will have failed. What could have gone wrong? What actions should we take today to avoid this?"

Consider practicing pre-mortems for the important projects in your life. For example, before your vacation to the other side of the country, you can ask yourself, "If this trip ended up in disaster, what could have caused it? Is there any preventive action I can take today?"

In particular, and here is where ergodicity and redistribution come into play, you could ask yourself the following question. "Is there any point of the vacation in which loads cluster together? Can I redistribute them?" For example, fatigue is a type of load. It might cluster during the 18-hours drive to the vacation spot. Falling asleep at the wheel or having a fight due to fatigue and stress are possible outcomes that might endanger the vacation and the relationship. The chances are that if something very bad happens during the holiday, it will happen where the load concentrates. A good idea might be to book an overnight stay mid-way, to redistribute the fatigue over two days.

BRITTLENESS

Earlier, we saw how hospitals break down when there is a spike in patients *and* they cannot redistribute them to other hospitals.

In mechanics, the inability to redistribute loads is called brittleness. Brittle materials, such as ceramic, break easily. This is because they cannot redistribute load spikes over their surface. A small hit, and they break. Conversely, ductile materials such as rubber and metal are more resistant. They can spread the load more evenly by deforming, whereas ceramics cannot.[77]

---

[77] What determines whether a material deforms or breaks under pressure is its capacity to redistribute load. It works like this. Imagine a ten-meters line on the ground, with ten dots, each one meter from each other. On each dot, stands a person. They all form a line, holding hands. Now, you take the largest dog you can find, and give the leash to one of the people. Finally, you throw a piece of meat far away.

When the dog runs towards the meat, he will pull on the leash. The person holding it will be pulled too, and he will begin pulling on the person(s) next to him. Two things might happen. One, the other 9 people prioritize staying on their dot. If the person with the leash pulls them away, they will release their hand, letting the him being carried away by the dog. The chain breaks. Two, the other 9 people don't care about staying on their dot and focus on holding hands together. They redistribute the force pulling on the leash between all of them, taking a few steps if needed. The chain doesn't break.

The first behavior – letting hands go rather than moving around and sharing the load – is what happens at a microscopic level in brittle materials, such as ceramic. Their grains (you can imagine them as groups of molecules) are stuck in a rigid structure, cannot move around, cannot deform, and thus cannot effectively share load. A small hit is all it takes to break them. If your grandma's ceramic vase falls from half a meter, it breaks.

Conversely, the second behavior – moving around and sharing the load rather than letting hands go – is what happens at a microscopic level in ductile materials, such as metals. Their grains deform and share the load. It's hard to break them. A metal bucket can fall from ten meters and not break.

In general, deformation helps with survival. For example, if you are free to shift your schedule around, you are better able to resist sudden spikes in workload. Or, if your commute can "deform" to another route, you can avoid traffic jams.

As another example, Amazon Web Services is a multibillion business based on the idea of selling computers[78] that can "deform" and expand their computing capacity when they receive load above average.

The point is, **to avoid breaking down, don't be brittle. Deform to accommodate your loads. More importantly, do not take too many commitments that prevent you from deforming.**

---

[78] Yes, it's more complex than that, I know. But the true nature of AWS is beyond the scope of this book.

PRACTICAL APPLICATION

As a freelancer, I learned that it is a good idea to keep some free time every week in case some overtime is required to meet a deadline. Otherwise, if something unexpected happens and I fail my deadline because I didn't have spare time to use, my client will be angry. He won't give a damn if next week I have free time.

It is not the average that matters, but the local. **Local spikes require local buffers.**

SUMMARY OF THIS CHAPTER

In this chapter, we have seen two concepts. One, redistributing loads helps to prevent irreversible losses. Two, redistribution of unexpected loads requires buffers or a local capacity to deform.

CHAPTER 6.2
FINANCIAL REDISTRIBUTION

Many people hold the idea that redistribution of resources is something that not only helps the worst performers but also harms the best ones. This is true in an ergodic world, but not in a non-ergodic one, not necessarily. **In a non-ergodic world, you often benefit from redistribution,** *even if you're giving more than you're receiving.* This phenomenon was so counterintuitive that I had to make a real-world example with numbers to believe it myself.

For example, imagine that both you and your friend Aaron are proposed the following game. You take turns shooting a basketball. If you make the basket, you double your money. If you fail, you halve it.

You are a better player than Aaron. Whenever you shoot, you have a 60% chance to make it. Aaron has only a 50% chance. What's the best strategy to maximize *your* gains (without caring about Aaron)?

Counterintuitively, if after both you and Aaron take a shot, the two of you decide to pool your money and take half, you will end up with more money than if you decided to play by yourself – even if you are a better shooter than Aaron.[79]

The next page explains why.

---

[79] This is an adaptation from the famous "Farmer's fable" thought experiment. The reason for the adaptation is that, in the fable, the two farmers have the same payoffs. Here, I wanted to show that even when one participant has higher payoffs than the others, it often pays to redistribute anyway.

RUNNING THE NUMBERS

Imagine that you make the first shot and miss the second one. You start with $100. After the first shot (in), you double it to $200. After the second shot (out), you halve it to $100. You end up with the same money with which you began.

Now, let's see what would have happened if you played with Aaron, and you made the first shot while he missed his, and then you missed your second shot while he made his. You both made one shot in and one out. If, after each shot, you polled your money and redistributed it half-half, the following happens.

You both begin with $100. After your first shot (in), you double your money to $200. After Aaron's first shot (out), he halves his money to $50. The two of you then poll your money, for a total of $250, and divide it half-half. Now, you both have $125. After your second shot (out), you half your money to $62.5. After Aaron's second shot (in), he doubles his money to $250. The two of you then poll your money, for a total of $312.5, and divide it half-half: you both have $156.25.[80]

The second scenario is much better for you than the first one! You end up with an extra $56.25! (I had to re-read the previous paragraph three times to convince me that it's actually what's going on.)

---

[80] Some readers might be interested in simulating outcomes and playing with redistribution using the (very rough) code at repl.it/@LucaDellanna/Ergodicity-Basketball#main.cs

This phenomenon occurs because, when wins and losses are reciprocal multiples of the bet, the absolute amount won is higher than the absolute amount loss. **It pays to redistribute, so that for each step forward, you only make a partial step back.**

REDISTRIBUTING PAYS EVEN IF YOU'RE BETTER

The phenomenon described above holds even if you are a better shooter than the person with whom you pool your money. Let's continue the experiment with you making the third shot, missing the fourth one, and making the fifth one, whereas Aaron does the opposite. In the end, three of your shots went in compared to two for Aaron: you shot better than him. In the scenario in which you do not redistribute, you end up with $200. If you redistribute, you end up with $305.

Redistributing pays, even if you're better than those with whom you redistribute.

There is not only an ethical rationale for redistribution, but a selfish one too.

LIMITATIONS AND OTHER CONSIDERATIONS

There are some limitations to the previous statement. If Aaron were a terrible player, missing all his shots, then you would be better off without redistributing with him. Moreover, the thought experiment assumes that you do not spend your wealth between games and that your two performances are not correlated. If it were the case, when you missed, he would also be likely to miss, nullifying the benefits of redistribution.

Another consideration could be that a 50-50 split is inefficient, and perhaps a 55-45 could be more efficient. Splitting 50-50 might induce laziness. Incentives matter.

That said, in general, **some redistribution is better than no redistribution.**

REDISTRIBUTION INCREASES ERGODICITY

The previous example showed how the problem with losses is not just that, well, you lost something. It's also that what you lost is not there anymore to generate returns for you.

For example, if you have $1000 to invest and lose $900 in a market downturn, when stocks double in price again, you will only have $200. The $900 you lost are not there anymore to double to $1800.

FULL AND PARTIAL IRREVERSIBILITY

There are two types of irreversibility.

The first one is what I call "game-over": death, bankruptcy, and so on. These are points of your life's trajectory that when you touch, you cannot leave ever again. This irreversibility is total.

The second type of irreversibility is partial. Some situations impair you and make a recovery hard but not impossible or cap your full potential but allow for partial recovery. For example, investing losses that do not cause bankruptcy, an injury that lets you exercise but not quite like before, and so on.

Redistribution helps mitigate both types of irreversibility. For example, unemployment benefits help avoid personal bankruptcy. The redistribution scheme in the basketball example above helps avoid excessive losses that are difficult to recoup.

Since irreversibility causes non-ergodicity, we can say that redistribution helps to decrease non-ergodicity.

As a reminder, in this book, I refer to ergodicity as a non-binary property. This is because of the practical reasons explained in Part 3. In Ergodicity Economics, instead, it is customarily intended as a binary property.

PRACTICAL APPLICATIONS

Here are some practical applications of redistribution:

- **Taxes,** obviously, but also other voluntary forms of financial redistribution within tight communities such as shared pools of money.[81] Also insurances and debt.

- **Sociality** is, in a way, a form of redistribution of time and care. I give you some of my time when I do not need it. In exchange, I get a chance to get some of your time when I need it.

- **Rebalancing a portfolio, sharing knowledge, playing positive-sum games, and reinvesting part of your finances in your community** are forms of redistribution. They help build direct and indirect safety nets that might benefit you in case your fortune would change.

---

[81] Note that unemployment benefits and public healthcare would fit in this category but not pensions – they are not a method to help individuals withstand short-term irreversibility.

INSURANCE

In their *Ergodicity Economics,* Ole Peters and Alexander Adamou show that insurances are a puzzle that expected values alone cannot solve.

Let's say that you have a house worth $100,000 and that there is a 1% possibility of it taking fire any given year. You are considering whether to buy insurance that would give you back the value of your house ($100,000) in case it burned down.

The expected yearly value of the insurance contract would be the value of the insured good ($100,000) multiplied by the chance of the insurance triggering (1%). The total is $1000.

The insurer would want more than $1000, to cover his operating costs. In contrast, the owner would be willing to pay $1000 at most. Since these two ranges do not overlap – more than $1000, and up to $1000 – we would expect insurance contracts never to be signed. In reality, they are common. So, something else must be going on.

Not insuring one's house means that a fire causes his owner to go bankrupt, unless he is very wealthy. In contrast, a single house taking fire doesn't cause its insurer to go bankrupt.

Therefore, the owner is willing to pay a premium to protect himself from irreversibility. **The insurer is willing to sell this protection from irreversibility because it increases his own exposure less than it decreases it for the owner.** This is because the insurer is wealthier than the house owner and can thus tolerate larger temporary losses without going bankrupt.[82]

ADDITIONAL NOTES ON INSURANCES

I simplified the previous example a lot. Ole Peters and Alexander Adamou offer a detailed and formal explanation in their paper "Ergodicity Economics."

Another way to grasp what is going on is to remember that (non)ergodicity is not just a property of an activity – in this case, insurance. Instead, it is a property of an actor, an activity, and the exposure of the former to the latter. Also, the value of an activity is seldom absolute. Often, it depends on who performs it and on the risks to which he is exposed. Any analysis that claims irrationality without considering these two points is likely to be flawed.

---

[82] Peters and Adamou explain it as, insurance allow for higher time-average growth rates, even though it appears to be the purchase of an expected loss.

OTHER BENEFITS OF REDISTRIBUTION

So far, we have only seen the direct benefits of redistribution. There are indirect ones too.

For example, it eases social tension, creates a stabler system, and fosters positive-sum games. These all bring indirect benefits to those redistributing.

ALTRUISM AND REDISTRIBUTION

As we saw in the previous pages, redistribution is full of benefits. I suspect that we evolved altruism as a way to produce redistributive behaviors.

LOCALISM AND ITS BENEFITS

Localism is the opposite of centralization. In a centralized country, decisions are taken by institutions at the country's geographical, cultural, and social center. These decisions are then applied equally to the whole country, with no tailoring.

Conversely, localism wants decision-making to happen at the lowest level possible. At the community level, if possible; if not, at the town level; if not, at the province level, and so on. This allows the decision-makers to know the topic of the decision closely, to have skin in the game so that they do not take excessive or unethical risks, and to make very tailored policies.

VARIANCE BENEFITS ERGODICITY

We already saw how populations benefit from the action of natural selection on some of its members.[83] On the other hand, populations want most of their members to survive, not just their fitter ones. This is for three reasons. One, we are humans. Two, numbers bring strength. Three, numbers bring variance, and variance is important.

As environments change and predators or competitors evolve, the traits required for thriving vary too. One day, the tribe might need someone strong. Another day, it might need someone smart. It is wise to preserve the smart even when his skills are not needed.[84]

Altruism and redistribution help to keep a population diverse and thus more resistant to the unknowns of the future.[85]

---

[83] Or components.

[84] In a related note, a major problem I see in the governments of some countries is a lack of variance.

[85] In centralization, redistribution follows the arc local → central → local. For example, my taxes go to the central government, which redistributes it to the regions, which redistribute it to the provinces, and so on. Conversely, in localism, redistribution follows the arc local → local, at least for the most part. For example, part of my taxes goes to my town that uses them for initiatives that improve my town and the life of its citizens.

This is good: someone who knows that his money will go to his town knows that he will benefit indirectly from his contribution. Therefore, he is more likely to contribute and might contribute more, further increasing the benefits for his community and for him.

This is not to say that redistribution should only happen locally. For some risks, redistribution is more effective at higher scales. For example, regions more affected by a pandemic benefit from the operational and financial help of other, less-affected regions.

CHAPTER 6.3

SUMMARY OF THE THIRD STRATEGY, REDISTRIBUTION

In general, redistribution within a system increases the ergodicity of its participants.[86]

We saw that in load distribution, the capacity to deform (i.e., redistribute load) allows the mitigation of load spikes that are often the trigger for irreversible damage.

We also saw how financial redistribution not only helps to avoid bankruptcy but also increases long-term outcomes *even* for those who are producing more than the average person.

---

[86] "In general," because there are exceptions. For example, extreme redistribution might cause incentive problems, moral hazards, or tragedies of the common.

Part 7

OTHER EXAMPLES OF NON-ERGODICITY

This last part of the book presents three more examples of non-ergodicity: behavioral change, the coronavirus pandemic, and investing.

CHAPTER 7.1
BEHAVIORAL CHANGE

If you manage to brush your teeth after dinner for thirty days straight, you're likely to have formed a lifetime habit. Conversely, if you brush them only once a week, you might go for your whole life without having formed a habit of brushing teeth.

Not only do habits take repetition, but they also take consistency. It's not about how many times you perform a habit. Instead, it's about how many times you perform it *within a short period*.

Behavioral change is non-ergodic. The distribution of efforts matters.

THE IMPORTANCE OF ACHIEVING CRITICAL MASS

I spend part of my time helping organizations build a culture of operational excellence. I have observed with my eyes hundreds of companies. I do not know of a single one that built desired habits without obsessing over it for a short period. If a manager can keep his team focused on getting one thing right for about 2-4 weeks, he will have created a lasting habit.

Conversely, I have seen many companies whose managers remind their workers about the desired behavior once a week for years. They obtain no result. Of course – they fail to achieve the critical mass required in the minds of their team members to build a habit.

Managers that ignore the non-ergodic nature of behavioral change end up wasting their time and achieve no result. Conversely, those who acknowledge it get quick successes that compound over time.

CHAPTER 7.2
ERGODICITY AND THE PANDEMIC

I wrote my first four books sitting at coffee shops. I'm writing this one from my kitchen table because it is 2020, and the recent coronavirus pandemic made it risky to spend hours in enclosed public spaces.

One reason why many countries mismanaged the pandemic is a misunderstanding of ergodicity. Here are some considerations that have been neglected.

- **"Number of cases per country" and "number of cases per country per 100,000 population" are less useful measures than apparent.** Sure, they tell us how many people are infected (assuming correct data and transparent communication – a strong assumption). However, they do not tell us much about the state of healthcare. From this point of view, "number of hospitals with bed saturation higher than 95%" would be a better measure. Moreover, they do not tell us much about containment. "Number of active clusters" would have been a better metric. The point is, we measure to make decisions, and these decisions should consider local conditions. National averages are misleading.

- **Ro.** This coefficient is supposed to tell us how infective the virus is. It estimates the expected number of cases directly generated by one case in a population where all individuals are susceptible to infection. From most practical points of view, it is useless at best and misleading at worst. First of all, it is not the property of just a virus – as the media depicted it. Instead, it is the property of a virus, a population, the quantity of the former in the latter, and the exposure of the latter to the former. For example, the same virus can have different Ro values depending on whether concerts are allowed. More importantly, as many pointed out, spending 120 minutes with a single friend has a different potential for contagion than spending 10 minutes with 12 friends. Again, averages are misleading.

- **The average mortality doesn't tell us much about the lethality of the virus.** There are two hypotheses related to this. One, proven in Northern Italy, that the distribution of the infections affects their mortality. If too many sick go to the same hospital, the staff cannot attend to them enough, and their mortality rises. The second hypothesis, speculative, is that how much virus you inspire determines its lethality. Under this assumption, it's important to know not only how many deaths and cases there have been but also their distribution. A virus that is spread homogeneously over a country seems less lethal than it really is.

- **Narrow forecasts on the number of deaths assume no path-dependency.** Given two identical countries, one which enacts preventive measures at the beginning of January and one that enacts them at the beginning of February will have a different number of deaths in March, all other things equal (because the virus got time to spread and the number of people within one "social distance" of an infected are higher in the second country). Any forecast that considers such path dependency is bound to have a large bracket of forecasted numbers. It follows that any forecast with a narrow range assumes no path-dependency – an extremely strong assumption.

These were just a few of the many ways in which analyses regarding the pandemic assumed that our world is ergodic when it isn't, producing misleading information.

CHAPTER 7.3
NARROWNESS, BROADNESS, AND ERGODICITY

At the beginning of this book, we saw that what is optimal to win a single race is not optimal to win a championship. Of course, both require skills and athleticism. But on top of that, a championship requires some sustainability. You cannot give it all and risk your life or your joints, not as much as you could if all that mattered was a single race.

The same can be said *within* a race. If you are one of the top ten skiers, it is relatively easy to be the fastest in a single slope. Just go down without caring about the next turn, your knees, or your life.

The easiest way to increase performance is to narrow the time frame over which it is measured.

Sadly, it is also the easiest way to produce unsustainable performance.

If your tactic to go faster is to do as if there were no negative consequences, you will go faster, and you will receive the negative consequences. It's probably not a trade-off worth making.

SUSTAINABLE PERFORMANCE

If you want to be a fast skier, it's very easy. Just keep your skis straight, your knees bent, and go down the slope as straight as possible. You will have a hard time avoiding a crash, but for a few seconds, you will be fast.

Everyone can be fast. The hard part is being fast while retaining control. The hard part is to be fast in the short term *and* the long term.

The easiest way to increase short-term performance is to do so at the cost of long-term performance. It is hardly a tradeoff you want to make. My cousin did it, and his career ultimately suffered from it.

Here are some other examples of the same tradeoff.

- Any salesperson can easily post record sales this month. The hard part is to do it without using discounts or deception, so that neither the brand nor the profits suffer.

- Most people can have a great career at something. The hard part is to do it while keeping a healthy personal life.

- Any restaurant manager can make it more efficient by buying cheaper ingredients. The hard part is to cut costs while keeping quality high.

RESTRICTING THE SCOPE

We can generalize the previous examples as follows.

The easiest way to increase performance is to restrict the scope of its definition. For example, we can restrict the definition of fast from "fast during a whole championship" to "fast in this particular slope." Or, we can restrict the definition of happiness from "a fulfilling career, a happy family, a good social life, and a healthy body" to "a prestigious job title" or "a coveted spouse."

In both cases, we make the outcome easier to achieve, but it also means less and will matter for a shorter time.

Moreover, we open the door to undesired consequences. Maximizing our speed not across the whole championship or even across the race but on one particular slope might lead to us going too fast and crashing shortly afterward. Optimizing our relationship choices, or even our life, to achieve a marriage with a spouse envied by our friends might lead to a quick divorce.

EXPANDING THE SCOPE

On the other hand, **the easiest way to hide problems is to increase the scope of measurement.**

If a town has a few districts whose population lives in poverty, it can conveniently hide the problem by talking about the average income measured across the city as a whole.

If your romantic life is in shambles, you can conveniently hide the problem by measuring your happiness across all your activities, including your career and your friends.

In the previous section, we saw how reducing the scope of measurement to increase performance opens the door to undesired consequences. Expanding the scope of measurement to hide problems leads to them too. **Problems grow the size they need for them to be acknowledged.** A hidden problem is a problem that keeps growing, and that will damage us more painfully in the future. For example, social unrest is not a problem for the wealthier part of the population until riots start, and ignored health problems grow to threaten our lives.

ERGODICITY AND SCOPE

Ergodicity provides us with a few tools to recognize whether, in a given context, it is safe to expand or restrict the scope of measurement. In general, in non-ergodic contexts, it is not safe to do so.

Whether a context is ergodic can tell us:

- If it is safe to optimize short-term performance, or whether we should care about securing sustainability first. Had my cousin known about ergodicity, he would have known that skiing each race as if it were the last one might actually make it become the last one.

- If it is safe to use averages, or whether we should consider more granular data. Had we known that, we would have managed the pandemic better (as described in a previous chapter).

- Why so many employees burn-out. A company cares about performance across all its employees in a given month, but an employee cares about his performance across his whole career. Different scopes create a conflict of interest for the employee and his employer, even if both care about the same metric, performance.

EFFICIENCY AND EFFECTIVENESS

The tension described above between short-term and long-term performance is similar to the difference between efficiency and effectiveness. When a skier goes down the hill at full speed, he is efficient. He only needs a few seconds to complete the slope. When a skier has a long career full of medals, he is effective.

The difference between efficiency and effectiveness is that the former is a snapshot in time, and the latter describes a lifetime. Or, to be more precise, efficiency is restricted by time (in that case, the duration of the race). In contrast, effectiveness is expanded across time, encompassing an entire lifetime. What is efficient in the short term might or might not be effective in the long term.

SUMMARY OF THIS CHAPTER

- The easiest way to increase performance is to restrict the scope of its definition. Sadly, it is also the easiest way to incur problems.

- The easiest way to hide problems is to expand the scope of measurement.

- Ergodicity determines whether it is safe to restrict or expand the scope of measurement.

CHAPTER 7.4
SUSTAINING PERFORMANCE

As I am writing these lines, legendary investor Warren Buffett is the seventh richest person on Earth. He made 99.7% of his fortune after his 52nd birthday and 30% of his fortune after his 83rd birthday.[87]

Of course, his skills in producing high returns mattered.[88] But his skills in avoiding bankruptcy mattered more.[89] If he had gone bankrupt before the age of 60, as many "brilliant" investors did, he would have been forgotten.

---

[87] At the moment of writing his book, Buffett is 90 years old. The first piece of data on him is dated 2018, the second, 2020.

[88] And so did his skills at being active in a secular bull market.

[89] Much of the returns of investing come from compounding – the fact that the returns of an investment produce returns of their own. For example, $100 invested in a venture that returns 10% a year yields $10 a year. However, if the returns are invested back in, the second year the yield will be $11, then $12.1, $15.8 after 30 years, and $106.7 after 50 years. It escalates quickly.

Being able to stay in the game for a long time pays a lot.

UNSUSTAINABLE PERFORMANCE

Energy company Enron has been awarded Fortune magazine's "America's most innovative company" award for six years between 1996 and 2001. It then filed for bankruptcy in the same year, 2001.

The problem with these awards is that they look at returns without also looking at sustainability. They look at who makes the most smoke, without checking if they're burning their house in the process.[90]

It is easy to make money. I could sell my kidney or scam a neighbor. It is much harder to do so in a way that doesn't fuck up my life.

In real life, consequences matter and are there to stay. **Sustainability is often a larger obstacle to performance than talent.** Few are willing to sacrifice their marriage, their health, their reputation, or anything else that, if lost, is hard or impossible to get back. As a result, they make conservative choices.

Are they really sacrificing returns by taking these conservative choices, though? Or are they maximizing them, all things considered?

---

[90] A naïve metaphor would be that of "regression to the mean." While technically and poetically correct, it misses the point that a company could be wildly successful *and* continue to be successful. One cannot dismiss an exceptional result as noise; one must prove that the underlying distribution of future outcomes for the company at hand is still a mediocre one.

A better remark would be that these awards are only based on lagging indicators – metrics that measure the past. Instead, a serious award would complement lagging indicators with leading ones – metrics that measure the fundaments of success.

LEADING AND LAGGING INDICATORS

Readers of my two books on management, "Best Practices For Operational Excellence" and "Teams Are Adaptive Systems," are familiar with my thoughts around indicators. Companies track indicators such as revenue, profit, and incidents. These are called *lagging* indicators, for they describe what already happened.

Conversely, some companies also track *leading* indicators. These measure the factors influencing the future performance of the company. For example, the behaviors expressed by the employees, their skills, the hours of training done, the number of clients visiting or visited, and so on.

There are many benefits to tracking leading indicators in addition to lagging ones. For example, suppose that you measure how many employees of your company wear personal protective equipment (a leading indicator). If you discover that many do not wear them, you have a chance to correct the situation before one of them gets injured. Conversely, if you estimate the safety of your workplace by only measuring incidents (a lagging indicator), you will only take action after the damage is done.

Measuring leading indicators allows you to spot problems before they get a chance to cause irreparable damage. Relaying on lagging indicators ensures that you will get hit by irreversibility, eventually. By now, the impact on the ergodicity of both should be clear.

ACHIEVING SUSTAINED PERFORMANCE

Most frustration comes from doing the necessary believing it is sufficient. Hence, let me clarify that the contents of this paragraph are not sufficient to achieve sustained performance but merely necessary – unless you rely on luck.

I believe that to achieve sustained performance, it is necessary to measure leading indicators. They will keep you on track, allowing you to outlast your competitors, even if they are more skilled or wealthier. They will give you chances to avoid game-overs. They will show you where what others call luck resides.

Conversely, relying on lagging indicators is not enough. They mislead the observer to go all-in during an ephemeral success, causing him to be destroyed by the following regression to the mean. They introduce a false sense of security by not measuring problems until they're big enough to cause irreparable damage, or by not spotting success until it is apparent (and therefore dissuading everyone but the most determined).

By giving you a chance to react to problems before they hurt you irreparably, leading indicators increase your ergodicity. Conversely, lagging ones decrease it.

Choose wisely what to measure.

CONCLUSIONS

In the first half of this book, I explained how mistaking a non-ergodic system for an ergodic one causes wrong decisions. In particular:

- In the first part of the book, I showed how irreversibility causes losses to absorb future gains.

- In the second part, we saw how systems can work on average and still fail locally, if losses are irreversible for its local components.

- In the third part, we learned that a system is non-ergodic if the lifetime outcomes of its participants do not coincide with the expected outcome.

Then, in the second half of the book, I described three strategies to manage non-ergodicity:

- The barbell strategy: avoid exposing all of yourself to a risk of ruin, no matter how small.

- Skin in the game: ensure that the dangerous gets removed, fast.

- Redistribution: it's good for you, even if you're above average.

The last few pages of this book contain quotable bits and information about me and my other books. Enjoy!

QUOTABLE BITS

When people say that childhood was the best time of their lives, they usually miss reversibility.

Avoiding the risks of ruin is how you get ahead in the long-term.

Maximizing the expected returns of your choices is a good strategy if and only if mistakes and misfortunes are reversible.

What is optimal in the presence of reversibility is stupid otherwise, and the other way around.

It is not the best ones who succeed. It is the best ones of those who survive.

Performance is subordinate to survival.

Over the short term, consequences that apply beyond the short-term do not matter. Over the long term, they do.

Irreversibility absorbs future gains.

Distinguish between calculated risks whose consequences you can recover from and recklessness whose consequences might permanently debilitate you. There is a sweet spot where you expose yourself to the former but not the latter – that's a good place to aim.

Any form of "game-over" nullifies future gains, bringing the average down.

For real people, the limitation on the number of times they can play can transform their lifetime outcome of a gamble to negative.

It is pointless to envy someone with whom you wouldn't trade places in all parallel universes.

Do not envy the survivors of ventures in which you didn't participate.

A system can work well on average and still fail locally.

As an individual, you do not care whether the system works on average. You care if it works for you.

Central organizations are only efficient to the central observer.

The best strategy depends on whether you are the gamble or the gambler.

The survival of a population does not coincide with the survival of its members, not all of them.

Whether you live in an ergodic world determines what is rational and what isn't.

For most people, what matters is how much their lifetime outcome diverges from the population outcome in the medium term.

Moods are tools to adapt to environments with clustered resources.

Moderately moody people tend to be more efficient than moodless ones.

Natural selection is inevitable, but we can avoid it at any given level by pushing it towards a lower one.

A population can decrease its exposure to irreversibility by exposing its members to it.

Systems that can instantaneously share load are more ergodic.

In a non-ergodic world, you benefit from redistribution even if you're giving more than you're receiving.

It pays to redistribute, so that for each step forward, you only make a partial step back.

Ergodicity is a property of an activity, its participants, and the exposure of the latter to the former.

Behavioral change is non-ergodic. The distribution of efforts matters.

Sustainability is often a larger obstacle to performance than talent.

The easiest way to increase performance is to narrow the time frame over which it is measured. Sadly, it is also the easiest way to produce unsustainable performance.

The easiest way to hide problems is to increase the scope of measurement.

Problems grow the size they need for them to be acknowledged.

ABOUT THE AUTHOR

An automotive engineer by training, after having led large teams and consulted for large multinationals, Luca quit his corporate job to become an independent researcher and author.

He dedicated his career to research the topic of emerging behavior and communicate its findings and their implications.

After having lived in Spain, Germany, Kazakhstan, and Singapore, Luca recently moved back to his hometown of Turin (Italy). He spends his days between consulting, teaching, and conducting his independent research from his home, a coffee bar, or a park.

Luca also consults corporations, startups, and individuals on behavioral change and antifragile operations. Once per year, he teaches a Risk Management module at Genoa University. He also regularly holds private workshops for entrepreneurs, operations managers, plant managers, and CEOs / COOs.

YOU CAN FIND LUCA ON…

Luca writes regularly on Twitter (**@DellAnnaLuca**). You can visit his professional website and blog at **www.luca-dellanna.com**. You can also contact him at **Luca@luca-dellanna.com**

At the end of this tome, you will find a brief overview of Luca's other books.

You can show your support to Luca by recommending this book to your friends or colleagues, by leaving a review on Amazon / Gumroad / Goodreads, or by contributing to his cause on Patreon (**patreon.com/dellannaluca**).

OTHER BOOKS BY LUCA DELLANNA

100 TRUTHS YOU WILL LEARN TOO LATE

"I am amazed at Luca Dellanna's ability to observe, compile, and articulate 99 very actionable life principles here. Each chapter describes the rule in a way that makes you think and then summarizes the action. It's filled with DEEP insights yet VERY readable."

– Theresia Tanzil

"Absolutely brilliant. You might have grasped some of these concepts before, but having them structured and in writing makes all the difference [...] I will surely recommend it to friends and co-workers."

– *Alberto Pisanello*

"A very thoughtful piece of writing, deep and wiring!"

– *David Krejca*

"Luca Dellanna's new book, "100 Truths," is super tight! [...] Practical, directional advice."

– *Hari Meyyappan*

"A thoughtfully written book in very straightforward language."

– *A.L. Peevey*

I wasted years of my life because I did not know its rules.

I did not know the rules of relationships, of careers, of health, of happiness.

Then, through hard work, talking with mentors, and trial and error, I uncovered some of them.

Now, I lay these rules out for you. In this book, you will find 100 of the lessons I learned.

It will still require hard work from your side to internalize them and put them into practice. Still, this book will make this process easier by letting you avoid committing the same mistakes I did.

THE CONTROL HEURISTIC, 2ND EDITION

"This book is like a magnificent suspension bridge, linking the science of the human brain to the practical craft of applying it in everyday life. I loved it." – Rory Sutherland

"A SUPERB book [...] by one of the profound thinkers in our field [behavioral economics]." – Michal G. Bartlett

"Luca's book was so helpful to my work. Opened my eyes up to some more reasons why change is so hard."
– Chris Murman on the first edition

At first look, human behavior appears as an inexplicable mess. Why do we behave irrationally? Why do *I* behave irrationally? Why is it so hard to change? What is happiness, and why does it seem to escape us?

We can only understand the brain as a distributed entity. The key to understanding it is to look at how the different brain regions interact with each other, how misunderstandings become illusions, and how selfish interests become irrational behaviors.

The Control Heuristic offers a new perspective to answer these questions. It provides a guiding light to shed the darkness of the subconscious resistances that prevent us from behaving like the man or woman we want to be.

TEAMS ARE ADAPTIVE SYSTEMS

"I'm a huge fan of High Output Management and Setting the Table [...] Luca's Best Practices for Operational Excellence took my management to the next level.

It's been almost a month since I started implementing the principles, but I can already say that I've noticed a significant improvement in my company's morale [...] That feels amazing."

– Molson Hart, Viahart CEO

If you manage teams, one of the hardest lessons you will have to learn is that your decisions are important not for their immediate result, but for the future behaviors they make more likely in your subordinates.

In my professional experience, I noticed that the best managers are those who understand that teams are adaptive systems.

Teams do not act but react. They learn not from words and speeches but from their work environment. They respond to the incentives that are communicated through action, not words.

When I see a manager struggling, it is often not because he doesn't make the right decisions based on what he knows, but because he cannot see the experiences that his subordinates are having and that shape their behavior.

In this book, I will teach you to see what your subordinates see, to understand how they adapt to your actions. Once you understand the pressures they are subject to, you will know what to do to shape their behavior and align their perceived incentives to what is good for the company and their professional development.

This book is the game-changer that transforms team management from a messy and noisy activity to a simple set of cause-effect relationships.

THE WORLD THROUGH A MAGNIFYING GLASS

"Thank you for helping me understand! My son was recently diagnosed, and I needed to be able to understand how he views the world. Why certain things would overwhelm him and cause so much anxiety and pain. This book made it so clear and easy to understand."
– Geiger T.

"Thanks to Luca Dellanna for his book about autism and ASD. It's probably one of the best works I have read in that matter (I have read a few), and it's surprising how realistically he depicts the condition."
– Manel Vilar

"Loved The World Through a Magnifying Glass – this analogy NAILS IT."

– Emerson Spartz, NYT Bestseller Author

This book is for parents, friends, or anyone related to someone with Autism.

This book is for neurologists and psychologists to help them understand the world of autism spectrum disorders.

This book is for people on the Spectrum, to help them understand themselves.

Some of the topics covered inside:

- The Magnifying Glass: a metaphor to understand perception under the Spectrum

- Why people on the Spectrum are impaired in contextual fields (such as personal communication) and advantaged in mastering detailed fields (such as computer science).

- Peripheral Functionality Blindness: the reason people on the Spectrum do not develop appropriate body language and facial expressivity.

- Prioritization by Specificity: the reason literal meaning is the only thing that matters for people on the Spectrum.

- The High-Pass filter: a novel hypothesis for the Autism Spectrum Disorder, coherent with previous theories and experimental results.

(Reading time is about 1h30)

THE POWER OF ADAPTATION

"This guy! Luca is amazing. So insightful with common-sense applications of complexity and the ability to communicate clearly!!" – Bob Klapetzky

This book is for you if:

- You like books dense with information.
- You appreciated books such as Taleb's *Antifragile*.
- You accept that the world is dynamic. Therefore, understanding how something changes is more important than understanding how something works now.
- You do not like usual business / self-help books that provide solutions that only work in the short-term.

"The Power of Adaptation" focuses on the topic of adaptation as the main force shaping the world as we know it. However, adaptation is an emergent process. Therefore, it cannot be understood through narratives, nor can it be acted upon directly. This book aims to describe the underlying phenomena which weave together into what we perceive as adaptation. It is a guide to practice **the four behaviors that will help them harness, rather than fight, change.**

BEST PRACTICES FOR OPERATIONAL EXCELLENCE

A book on Operations Management for CEOs, COOs, and Operations Managers.

Written by an author who understands complex systems and how to design antifragile operations.

Inside:

- The Four Principles of Operational Excellence.
- The Eight Best Practices of Operational Excellence.
- How to roll-out and sustain a change initiative.

ACKNOWLEDGMENTS

To my wife, Wenlin Tan, for the love and joy she brings to my life.

To my mother, for supporting and loving me all my life, and to Franco, for loving her. To my father, for the same and for stirring intellectual curiosity within me.

To my family in law, for having raised my love and having taken care of me while I was at their house.

To my friends and everyone else who, directly or indirectly, knowingly or unknowingly, contributed to my well-being.

To my Patrons Ross Screaton, Malcolm Ocean, Ricardo Ortiz Noguera, Michael Hart, Kimmo Kontra, Georges Piva, Jason Hunter Watson, Dhananjay, Mate Wohlmuth, Trevor Bragdon, Pablo Cárdenas, and Eric Anderson. Their help gave me stability on top of which I could conduct my research.

This book wouldn't have seen the light without the previous work on ergodicity of many scholars. Nassim Nicholas Taleb, Ole Peters, Alexander Adamou, Murray Gell-Mann, Ed Thorp, John Larry Kelly Jr., Joseph Norman, and all the other scholars who worked on the topic. This book stands on the shoulders of giants.

Unless noted otherwise, all images come from Pixabay, Unsplash, or Wikimedia Commons.

FURTHER READINGS

"Ergodicity Economics," by Ole Peters and Alex Adamou. The technical text of reference, in my opinion. I also recommend reading the other papers by the same authors.

"Skin in The Game" and "Antifragile," by Nassim Nicholas Taleb, on many of the topics discussed in this book.

"The Dynamics of Risk-Taking," by Luca Dellanna (myself), on how damage propagates, how it becomes irreversible, and dynamic considerations.

"Ergodicity and Digital Culture," by Frédéric Prost, on how ergodicity influences the spread of cultures.

"The Precautionary Principle (with Application to the Genetic Modification of Organisms)," by Nassim Nicholas Taleb, Rupert Read, Raphael Douady, Joseph Norman, and Yaneer Bar-Yam.

Printed in Great Britain
by Amazon

56367539R00095